COLLINS GEM

WORLD RECORDS

Elaine Henderson

HarperCollins*Publishers*

The author would like to thank the following for their
help and advice in the compilation of this book:
Mat Wheeler; Dr David Henderson; Meteorological
Office; Mitchell Library, Glasgow; National Power;
North of Scotland Water Authority; Wind Energy Group.

HarperCollins Publishers
P.O. Box, Glasgow G4 0NB

First published 1998

Reprint 10 9 8 7 6 5 4 3 2 1 0

© HarperCollins Publishers 1998

Collins Gem® is a registered trade mark of
HarperCollins Publishers Limited

ISBN 0 00 472177-2

Printed and bound in Great Britain by
Caledonian International Book Manufacturing Ltd, Glasgow, G64

Contents

Introduction

Some are born record makers, some set out to become record makers and some make the record books whether they intend to or not! If you're born a cheetah you're automatically the fastest sprinter in the world, and if, like Andy Green, you succeed in breaking the world land speed record then (at least for the time being!) you're assured of membership of that most exclusive club, the world record-holders. And again, there are those people like Alexander Graham Bell and Edward Jenner whose passionate devotion to their work and faith in themselves resulted in some of the most important scientific, technological and medical discoveries without which our modern world would be inconceivable.

In this little book we bring together over 500 different records from across the range of natural attributes, feats, endeavours and achievements, collected under the broad headings of Natural World, Space, Science, Technology and Communication, Human Life, the Arts, and so on. Here you can find the oldest living thing in the world, the coldest planet, who printed the first book and where to find the longest bridge.

To the best of our knowledge all information is correct at the time of going to press but such is the astonishing speed of contemporary progress and scientific discovery, that new records are being set daily. We know more about our world today than ever before but such is the human capacity for curiosity and the world's equally inexhaustible ability to surprise us, that the definitive list of 'world records' may never be compiled!

Earth

Highest mountain
Mt Everest, Tibet/Nepal
29,028 ft (8848 m)

Everest lies in the Himalayan range on the Tibet/Nepal border (Tibet is now also known as Xizang, a Chinese province). It was first seen by Europeans in the 1850s when British mapmakers spotted a tiny white peak among the mountain tops in the far distance. Theodolite readings were taken and Peak XV was pronounced the highest in the world. In 1856 it was named after Sir George Everest, who led the Great Trigonometrical Survey which resulted in the first accurate maps of the area. Its Tibetan name, *Chomdungma*, translates as 'mother goddess of the world'. The mountain was not scaled until 1953, when a British expedition, led by New Zealander Edmund Hillary and Sherpa Tensing Norgay, reached the top. By 1986 more than 300 teams had successfully reached the summit, five without oxygen. Scaling Everest still seems to exert an irresistible appeal for climbers, although many people have died, and continue to die, in the attempt. The weather on Everest is notorious for its unpredictable nature and can deteriorate without warning leaving climbers very vulnerable.

Highest mountain in Europe
Mont Blanc, French/Italian border
15,771 ft (4807 m)

Mont Blanc ('White Mountain') is in the Alps and was first climbed in 1786 by Michel-Gabriel Paccard and Jacques Balmat. Its peak is in French territory and Chamonix, which lies in the valley below, has developed into the largest Alpine tourist centre and resort. The Mont Blanc tunnel, bored through the mountain, was opened in 1962; it is $7^1/_4$ miles (11.7 km) long.

Highest mountain in the UK
Ben Nevis, Scotland
4406 ft (1343 m)

Ben Nevis lies near Fort William in the Highlands of Scotland. Parts of the mountain are covered with snow all year.

Highest mountain in North America
Mt McKinley, Alaska, USA
20,320 ft (6194 m)

Mt McKinley lies in the Denali National Park; Denali is the original Athapascan Indian name for the mountain and means 'The Great One'. It was first climbed in 1913.

Highest mountain in South America
Aconcagua, Argentina
22,834 ft (6960 m)

Aconcagua lies in the northern Andes mountains, with its peak in Argentinian territory. It is of volcanic origin, but is not itself a volcano. Aconcagua was first climbed in 1897 by Matthias Zurbriggen.

Highest mountain in Africa
Kilimanjaro, Tanzania
19,340 ft (5895 m)

Kilimanjaro is an extinct volcano and snow-capped all year although, astonishingly, it is only 200 miles (320 km) from the equator. It was first climbed by Hans Meyer and Ludwig Purtscheller in 1889.

Highest mountain in Asia
Mt Everest, Tibet/Nepal
29,028 ft (8848 m)

See Highest mountain, p.6.

Highest mountain in Australasia
Mt Cook, New Zealand
12,349 ft (3764 m)

Mt Cook lies in New Zealand's South Island and is permanently snow-clad. The first sighting by Europeans was made in 1642 by the Dutch navigator, Abel Tasman. Its original Maori name was *Aorangi* or 'Cloud Piercer' but it was later renamed after Captain James Cook, the explorer, and now forms the central feature of Mt Cook National Park. It was first climbed in 1894.

Highest volcanic peaks
Hawaiian Islands
29,500 ft (9000 m) from the seabed to the peak

The Hawaiian Islands are formed from the peaks of huge lava piles which rise from the Pacific ocean floor to above sea level. The tops of these volcanic mountains form eight major islands and 124 islets.

Highest sea cliffs
Hawaii 3314 ft (1010 m)

Longest cave
Mammoth Cave,
Kentucky, USA 329 miles (530 km)

Mammoth Cave is part of the Flint Ridge Cave
System and was discovered in 1799. It is composed
of many interconnecting passages and spreads over
five different levels. The flow of the Echo river
which runs through it continues to wear away the
rock and make the cave system even larger. The
river is the habitat of a species of blind fish, found
nowhere else in the world. The fish, *Amblyopsis
spelaea*, are about 4 in (10 cm) long, have small, but
non-functional eyes, and touch receptors all over
the body and head. They are, therefore, perfectly
equipped to 'feel' rather than to see what is
around them in a completely black environment
where vision would be of no use. Cave systems
elsewhere support two other species of blind fish
found only in the USA.

Longest cave in the UK
Ease Gill, England
32$^1/_2$ miles (52.5 km) explored length

Deepest cave
Jean Bernard, France
5036 ft (1535 m)

Deepest cave in the UK
Ffynnon Dhu, Wales
1010 ft (308 m)

Largest cave
Sarawak Chamber, Sarawak, Malaysia
2297 ft (700 m) long, 1312 ft (400 m) wide,
230 ft (70 m) high

Longest stalactite
Poll an Ionana, Republic of Ireland
20 ft 6 in (6.2 m) long

Stalactites and stalagmites are formed in caves from the slow trickle and evaporation of mineralized water. The water leaks through the cracks in the rock and gathers up minerals which are then deposited elsewhere when the water evaporates. Stalactites, which grow downwards from cave roofs, are formed from layers of calcium carbonate. They are found mainly in limestone caves where they build up over thousands of years, undisturbed by wind, weather or the activities of humans.

Tallest stalagmite
Krásnohorská Cave, Czech Republic
105 ft (32 m)

Stalagmites grow upwards from the cave floor and can reach greater lengths than the more fragile stalactites.

Largest saltwater lake
Caspian Sea, Azerbaijan/Iran/Kazakhstan/ Russia
149,200 miles^2 (386,400 km^2)

The Caspian Sea was once joined to the Black and Aral Seas, thereby making a much larger area of water. The Caspian Sea was formed as the earth's crust rose and it was cut away from the rest of the water (its surface is now 92 ft (28 m) below the level of the Black Sea). The sea is fed by the Volga river (largest in Europe) and is tideless. It was once famed for its sturgeon, from which caviar is produced, but the reduced flows from the Volga, resulting from increased upstream agricultural irrigation and diversion into reservoirs, has greatly diminished the number of sturgeon the sea can support. In some places the Caspian Sea reaches depths of some 2500 ft (750 m).

Largest natural freshwater lake
Lake Superior, Canada/USA
31,700 miles² (82,100 km²)

Lake Superior is one of the five Great Lakes which border Canada and the USA and, together, cover the same area as the entire United Kingdom. Lake Superior lies about 600 ft (180 m) above sea level and has an average depth of some 475 ft (145 m).

Largest natural freshwater lake in the UK (area)
Loch Lomond, Scotland
120 miles² (312 km²)

Loch Lomond lies northwest of Glasgow and is one of Scotland's best known and most picturesque lochs. There are about 30 islets in the loch, the maximum depth of which is 625 ft (190 m) and it is much used by fishermen and boating enthusiasts. Climbers can see as far as the Grampian Mountains from the summit of Ben Lomond, a height of 3192 ft (972 m), on the east side of the loch.

Largest natural freshwater lake in the UK (volume)

Loch Ness, Scotland
23 miles (36 km) long, 788 ft (240 m) deep

Loch Ness lies in the Great Glen, the rift that bisects the Highlands of Scotland. It is fed by several rivers and flows out via the River Ness to the Moray Firth. The 'Loch Ness Monster' stories date back to the seventh century. Long-held beliefs that the loch is bottomless have been proved to be unfounded, although biologists suggest that, if it exists, the 'monster' could be a descendant of a pair of plesiosaurs, somehow trapped when the loch was cut off from the sea in the last Ice Age; the depth of the loch, temperature and food available would have ensured their survival. Most 'sightings' have occurred from the vantage point of 12th-century Urquhart Castle on the loch shore.

Deepest natural freshwater lake

Lake Baikal, Russia
Up to 5000 ft (1525 m)

Lake Baikal contains about one fifth of the earth's fresh water.

Deepest natural freshwater lake in the UK
Loch Ness, Scotland
788 ft (240 m)

See Largest natural freshwater lake, p.14.

Longest gorge
Grand Canyon, USA
280 miles (450 km)

The Grand Canyon, Arizona, was formed by the Colorado river which runs through it. Over billions of years the river has cut through the rock to a depth of 5900 ft (1800 m) exposing several different layers of rock and giving a complete geological history. The rocks at the base of the canyon are older than 570 million years, formed in the time when the only living creatures were single-celled organisms in the oceans. The canyon is now the centrepiece of a national park, but increasing pressure from tourism has led to concerns about environmental damage.

Best-known gorge in the UK
Cheddar Gorge, England

Cheddar Gorge takes its name from the village of Cheddar, famous for its cheese, and is situated in the Mendip Hills in Somerset. The vertical limestone cliffs are over 400 ft (120 m) high and run for 2 miles (3 km). Stone Age tools and bones have been found in the caves, which are used by about 100 Greater Horseshoe bats for winter hibernation. During the winter of 1997/8, central heating and a security grille were installed in their favourite roosting places to protect this rare bat, whose numbers nationally have dwindled to some 5000.

Longest river
Nile
4132 miles (6650 km)

The Nile flows through Tanzania, Uganda, Sudan and Egypt on the way from its source in the mountains of Burundi to the delta on the Egyptian coast. Water flows into the river from nine countries and three principal rivers – White Nile, Blue Nile and Atbara. The British explorer, John Hanning Speke, reached the source of the Nile, the Victoria Nile, flowing out of Lake Victoria in Uganda, in 1862. Ninety-nine per cent of Egypt's population lives either in the Nile delta or the Nile valley, and early Egyptian civilization was based along the Nile. The construction of the Aswan High Dam and Lake Nasser in the 1960s has cut the flow of water to the Nile delta, and this has brought unforeseen problems. There is now less sediment in the water, resulting in lower land fertility and wearing away of the delta lands, allowing salt water to encroach upon, and ruin, bordering farmlands.

Longest river in Europe
Volga
2193 miles (3529 km)

The Volga rises in the Valdai Hills, northwest of Moscow, and flows into the Caspian Sea (see above, Largest saltwater lake). Sixty per cent of the river's water comes from snow. The river basin occupies some 533,000 miles^2 (1,380,000 km^2), and much of Russia's economy is connected with the river, with a large proportion of the population living within reach of its banks. In addition, the Volga plays a central role in Russian national consciousness and folklore; known as 'Mother Volga', the river features strongly in song, story and folk memory.

Longest river in the UK
Severn
200 miles (322 km)

The Severn rises near the River Wye and flows out to the Bristol Channel and the Atlantic Ocean. It has 17 tributaries, more than any other British river, and drains an area of some 4350 miles^2 (11,266 km^2).

The Severn estuary is noted for its tidal bore – a high, steep wave caused by the incoming tide.

Longest river in North America
Mackenzie-Peace
2635 miles (4241 km) total length

The Mackenzie rises from the Great Slave Lake in the Northwest Territories and flows northward to the Beaufort Sea of the Arctic Ocean. The Finlay river, its farthest headstream, flows into the Peace River Reservoir. The Mackenzie-Peace system runs through Canada's remote and sparsely populated north country.

Longest river in South America
Amazon
4000 miles (6437 km)

The Amazon rises in the Peruvian Andes and flows through northern Brazil to the Atlantic Ocean. It has more than 1000 tributaries and it is estimated that 20% of all the water that runs off the surface of the earth becomes part of the river. The Amazon's drainage basin is almost double the size of that of any other river, and its estuary is about 167 miles (270 km) wide. The river is navigable by fairly large ships for about 1000 miles (1609 km) upriver from the Atlantic, and it has therefore formed a vital part of the economic development of the countries through which it flows. The forested lowlands beside the river are rich in plant and wildlife and very fertile. The opening up of this land for agriculture has led to the displacement of the indigenous Indian people and serious threats to the continuing survival of several species of wildlife.

Longest river in Africa
Nile
4132 miles (6650 km)

See Longest river, p.16.

Longest river in Asia
Yangtze
3400 miles (5472 km)

Also known as Ch'ang Chiang or Chang Jiang, the Yangtze rises on the Plateau of Tibet in western China, and flows through 12 Chinese provinces and regions before it reaches its delta on the East China Sea. The river's basin is known as the 'granary of China' because of its rich and fertile farmlands, and food from the Yangtze basin makes up half the country's agricultural output. The river is also China's chief inland waterway and large cities, such as Wuhan and Nanking, have been built along its shores, while Shanghai is on a tributary close to the Yangtze's estuary.

Longest river in Australasia
Murray
1609 miles (2589 km)

The Murray river lies between New South Wales and Victoria in Australia, and flows through the Snowy Mountains to the Indian Ocean. In recent years, irrigation measures and the building of reservoirs have reduced the amount of water in the river, leading to salinity problems. This is particularly worrying for the people who live in the city of Adelaide, which is dependent on the river for water. The Murray was named after Sir George Murray, a British Colonial Secretary.

Highest waterfall
Angel Falls (Churún Merú), Venezuela
3212 ft (979 m) total height, 2560 ft (780 m) highest uninterrupted drop

The Angel Falls (Salto Angelo) were named after the American pilot, Jimmy Angel, who first recorded them as he flew over the top in 1933.

These inaccessible and remote falls are made by the waters of the Churún river as it pours down the sheer sides of Devil's Mountain (Auyan-Tepui), the top of which is usually hidden by cloud.

Highest waterfall in Europe
Utigardsfossen Falls, Norway
2625 ft (800 m)

The water in the Utigardsfossen Falls comes from the Josterdal Glacier. Waterfalls are created when rivers flow for thousands of years over bands of soft and hard rock. The river wears away the softer rock more quickly and where the different types of rock meet, the river will plunge over the side. In terms of the geological timescale, waterfalls are temporary features of the landscape. For example, Niagara Falls has moved about $7^1/_2$ miles (12 km) upstream in the past 12,000 years through gradual erosion of the bedrock above the Falls.

Largest waterfall (by volume)
Chutes de Khone (Khone Falls),
Kampuchea/Laos
230 ft (70 m) high, 2,500,000 gallons (9,500,000 litres) per second, estimated flow

Largest glacier
Lambert Glacier, Antarctica
250 miles (402 km)

Glaciers are sheets of ice, formed when the winter snowfall exceeds the summer melt. Excess snow accumulates and gradually becomes transformed into ice. Each year the same process allows the ice mass to grow and it also becomes tougher and harder. Most, but not all, glaciers move. Glacial ice has had a great influence on the earth's geography: most of the great river systems originated in glaciers and around three quarters of the world's entire supply of fresh water is stored in the form of glacial ice. Over 10% of the earth's surface is permanently covered by ice. The melting of glaciers, as a result of 'global warming', has potentially serious implications for climate and weather patterns.

Fastest-moving glacier
Rinks Isbrae, Greenland
90 ft (28 m) per day

Glaciers usually move quite slowly, but they may occasionally have surges of speed. In 1963/4, for example, Brúarjökull Glacier in Iceland moved 410 ft (125 m) per day for over two months.

Largest desert
Sahara, Africa
3,320,000 miles^2 (8,600,000 km^2)

The Sahara occupies one quarter of the African continent and stretches from the Atlantic Ocean to the Red Sea, bordering 11 countries. Its name means 'wilderness' in Arabic. The Saharan landscape is diverse and includes flat tablelands, high mountains and sandy dunes, while the surface varies from fine sand to stones and rounded pebbles. Plants and animals are specially adapted to survive in conditions which combine high daytime temperatures with cool nights, and an average annual rainfall of less than 5 in (12.5 cm). Trees that can survive here include date palm, acacias and tamarisk. Today, around two million people, both nomads and settled, live in and around the Sahara; settled people usually live near the streams in the hilly country or by oases. Artesian wells have been constructed to tap water from great depths to provide sufficient for basic human needs and subsistence farming. The desert also holds oil deposits and other minerals. Rock paintings, some 6000 years old, have been discovered in the Sahara, showing that it was once a fertile place, home to elephants and cattle.

Largest ocean
Pacific Ocean
Up to 10,700 miles (18,115 km) at greatest width

The Pacific is twice the size of the Atlantic Ocean and has a greater area than all the land surfaces of the world put together. The ocean stretches from the Bering Straits on the Arctic Circle to Cape Adare, Antarctica. It is probably the world's oldest ocean, estimated to be some 600 million years old. However, it was the last of the world's great oceans to be discovered by Europeans. Ferdinand Magellan made the first voyage across the Pacific in 1520/21 and named it Pacific ('peaceful'). The greatest Pacific explorer was the British seafarer Captain James Cook, who undertook three expeditions between 1768 and 1779. By the end of the 18th century, most of the thousands of Pacific islands had been located and mapped.

Deepest ocean
Pacific Ocean
Mean depth 14,040 ft (4280 m), greatest depth 36,200 ft (11,034 m)

The deepest point of the Pacific so far discovered is the Marianas Trench, a depression in the ocean floor near the Mariana Islands. The trench stretches for more than 1580 miles (2543 km) at an average width of 43 miles (69 km) and has been measured as deep as 36,200 ft (11,034 m) near the island of Guam. In 1960, Jacques Picard recorded the deepest-ever dive, in his father's bathyscaphe *Trieste*, by going as far as 35,800 ft (10,911 m) into the trench.

Largest sea
Arabian Sea
1,491,000 miles^2 (3,862,000 km^2)

The Arabian Sea forms the northwest section of the Indian Ocean, bounded by India, Pakistan, Iran, the Arabian Peninsula and the Horn of Africa. Depths exceed 9,800 ft (2987 m) and it supports a rich and varied marine life, with plentiful tuna, sardine and shark. The Arabian Sea once formed part of a vital trade route between Europe and India.

Highest wave
110 ft (34 m)

This wave was reported by the United States ship *Ramapoo* during bad weather in the North Pacific in 1933. 'Freak waves' are caused by the collision of two sets of waves travelling in opposite directions. The highest such wave instrumentally recorded was

85 ft (26 m) by the British ship *Weather Reporter* in the North Atlantic in December 1972.

Highest tsunami
115 ft (35 m)

Tsunamis are also called seismic waves and tidal waves, although they have little to do with tides. They are, in fact, usually caused by earthquakes, especially those that disturb the ocean floor. Tsunamis can travel long distances at enormous speeds (up to 500 mph/805 km/h) and pose no threat in open seas, rising only to about 3 ft (1 m) high. However, as they slow down in shallow waters they suddenly surge to enormous heights – some have even been known to lift up entire ships. They then crash down on the land, destroying everything in their path. The highest tsunami ever recorded followed the Krakatoa earthquake in 1883 and is thought to have killed some 36,000 people on the neighbouring islands of Java and Sumatra. See Most powerful volcanic eruption, p.32.

Largest island
Greenland
840,000 miles^2 (2,175,600 km^2)

Greenland lies in the north Atlantic Ocean, with two-thirds of the island within the Arctic Circle. Its nearest major European neighbour is Iceland (about 200 miles/320 km away), but the smaller Ellesmere Island (which belongs to Canada) is closer, some 16 miles (26 km) distant. Greenland's principal feature is its massive ice sheet, second only to that of Antarctica in size, which extends for over 700,000 miles^2 (1,813,000 km^2), almost 85 per cent of the country's total land mass. Glaciers associated with the ice sheet include Jakobshavn Glacier, one of the world's fastest-moving glaciers at approximately 100 ft (30 m) per day. Greenland is a Danish dependency and the population is a mixture of Danish immigrants and native Greenlanders (Inuit or Eskimo). The economy is based on fishing, mining and the breeding of sheep and reindeer. Hunting for seal, polar bear and fox continues in the north. The capital is Nuuk, the only sizeable town, and the entire population numbers just 56,000.

Highest temperature recorded
136 °F (57.8 °C)
Al' Aziziah, Libya, 13 September 1922 and San Louis, Mexico, 11 August 1933

Highest temperature recorded in the UK
98.8 °F (37.1 °C)
Cheltenham, Gloucestershire, England,
3 August 1990

August 1990 was the warmest August since records began in 1659. This temperature broke the previous record of 98.1 °F (36.7 °C) in 1911. The summer of 1990 was marked by a heatwave which, directly and indirectly, caused several drownings, house fires, deaths among old people (heart attacks and strokes), property damage through subsidence, significantly higher levels of air pollution and algal growth in ponds and lakes, and serious insect infestations.

Lowest temperature recorded
-128.56 °F (-89.2 °C)
Vostok Base, Antarctica, 21 July 1983

Lowest temperature recorded in the UK
-17 °F (-27.2 °C)
Braemar, Scotland, 11 February 1895 and
10 January 1982

Hottest inhabited place
Dalol, Ethiopia
Average annual temperature 94 °F (34.4 °C)

Highest annual rainfall
444 in (1110 mm)
Mt Waialeale, Kauai, Hawaii

On average it rains 360 days out of 365 on Mt Waialeale.

Greatest rainfall in one calendar month
366.14 in (9150 mm)
Cherrapunji, India, July 1861

Greatest rainfall in one day
73.62 in (1840 mm)
Cilaos, Isle de Réunion, 16 March 1952

Greatest rainfall in one minute
1.23 in (30 mm)
Unionville, Maryland, USA

Highest annual rainfall in UK
257 in (6430 mm)
Sprinkling Tarn, Cumbria, 1954

Greatest rainfall in one day in UK
11 in (280 mm)
Martinstown, Dorset, 18 July 1955

Lowest annual rainfall
0.03 in (0.008 mm)
Arica, Chile

Driest place (longest drought)
Atacama Desert, Chile

The Atacama Desert forms part of the Atacama region of Chile, bounded on the east by Argentina and on the west by the Pacific Ocean. The desert is about 600–700 miles (966–1126 km) long and forms part of the dry Pacific shoreline. Its extreme climate is caused by thermal inversion: the Humboldt (Peru) Current in the Pacific causes cold air to remain at the surface of the water with stable warmer air above. This produces fog and cloud over the desert, but no rain. Some meteorological stations in the area have never recorded any rain at all, although heavy rains are known to fall between two and four times each century.

Largest clouds
Cumulonimbus up to 6 miles (9.7 km) high

Clouds of this magnitude would contain up to half a million tons (508,000 tonnes) of water.

Highest recorded wind speed
231 mph (371 km/h)
Mt Washington Observatory, New Hampshire,
USA, 12 April 1934

Fastest gust of wind in the UK
153 mph (246 km/h)
Cairngorm, Scotland, 20 March 1986

Fastest winds on earth
Up to 300 mph (483 km/h)
Winds of these speeds are found inside the funnels
of tornados.

Heaviest hailstones
2.20 lb (1 kg)
Gopalganj, Bangladesh, 1986
Over 90 people were killed in this hailstorm, which
also caused considerable damage to property.
Hailstones are formed in thunderclouds: the air
currents push water droplets upwards to the top of
the cloud, where they freeze in the cold air. The
droplets then fall down, accumulating additional
layers of freezing water as they go. Currents may
then force them up again to the top of the cloud,

where they harden further before falling again, and this process can be repeated several times until the hailstone finally falls to earth. The largest recorded hailstone in the UK weighed 5.25 oz (150 g). In 1984 in Munich, Germany, a violent hailstorm damaged 100,000 properties, 200,000 vehicles and 20 aircraft. In September 1988, a hailstorm in China injured 2000 people.

Largest piece of ice to fall to earth
20 ft (6 m) diameter
Ord, Scotland, 13 August 1849

Largest recorded snowflake
15 in x 8 in (38 cm x 20 cm)
Fort Keogh, Montana, USA, 28 January 1887

Most powerful volcanic eruption
Krakatoa, Indonesia, 26/27 August 1883

Krakatoa is a small mountainous island in the Sunda Strait, between Sumatra and Java, Indonesia. The volcano was generally considered to be safe as the only previous records of any disturbance dated from 1680. In the three months leading up to the eruption, there had been rumblings and puffs of smoke, but no-one could have foreseen the events that began at 1 pm on 26 August 1883 when the island, literally, started to explode. Within one hour Krakatoa was enveloped in a black cloud 17 miles (27 km) high, and within 24 hours a large part of the island seemed to have blown up and disintegrated. Explosions were heard in Australia, some 2000 miles (3219 km) away; ash was sent 50 miles (80 km) up into the air, falling on ships at sea and setting fire to rigging and to decks. Sulphurous winds blew across the water, causing strange, glowing flames to flicker round the masts of ships, known as St Elmo's Fire. The air for miles was choked with burning ash and supercharged with static electricity, and huge lightning bolts terrified sailors at sea. Tsunamis or seismic waves (see above, Highest tsunami) struck Java and other islands, causing death and destruction. Darkness fell for two and a half days over the whole region. Volcanic dust continued to drift around the earth several times for months afterwards, causing spectacular sunsets. The Krakatoa eruption was the first time the short and long term effects of a major volcanic eruption were scientifically studied.

Worst volcanic eruption in the 20th century
Mt Pelée, Martinique, 5/8 May 1902

Martinique, in the West Indies, was a French colony in 1902. Its main crop was sugar and the principal town, St Pierre, a picturesque place only 6 miles (10 km) from the volcano. On 5 May, lava flow from the volcano, some 4430 ft (1350 m) high, increased significantly. The people began to panic but the governor called out the army and restored order. He was anxious to prevent people from leaving the island because there was an election on 10 May and he wanted to make sure of the vote. In the event the election never took place since he, and everyone else, was dead by then. At 7.50 am on 8 May, the explosions began, followed by an avalanche of burning gas and ash, known as a *nuée ardente* (glowing cloud), surging towards St Pierre at around 115 mph (185 km/h). Over 30,000 people died. Only two are known to have survived; one, ironically a convicted murderer, was imprisoned in a windowless cell and escaped with severe burns.

Highest active volcano
19,876 ft (6060 m)
Cotopaxi, Ecuador

Highest active volcano in Europe
10,899 ft (3323 m)
Mt Etna, Sicily, Italy

Tallest geyser
195–380 ft (60–115 m),
Old Faithful, Yellowstone National Park,
Wyoming, USA

'Geyser' is derived from the Old Icelandic *geysir* meaning 'to gush forth'. Geysers are found in volcanic regions in the USA, Iceland and New Zealand and are produced by the heating of deep, underground waters. When the subterranean waters reach a temperature higher than boiling point, they produce steam which rises up through the earth and forces out the water above it. There are over 3000 geysers and hot springs in Yellowstone. 'Old Faithful' erupts every hour for about five minutes each time.

Worst earthquake
Upper Egypt/Syria, 1201

Over one million people are thought to have died in this earthquake, estimated at IX on the Mercalli Scale*. Earthquakes are explained by plate

* Mercalli Scale – the 12 degrees of intensity (I–XII) indicate the amount of damage caused: XII = total destruction.

35

tectonics: the earth's crust is composed of large, rigid plates that move; where two plates converge, known as a fault line, severe pressures are built up, until the stress is so great that the rocks split and shift.

Worst earthquake in the 20th century
Tangshan, China, 28 July 1976

The earthquake struck directly beneath the city of Tangshan at a depth of about 7 miles (11 km). Most of the buildings were not reinforced against shock and thousands were killed and buried beneath them. It is estimated that around 250,000 people died during the earthquake and its aftershocks. The Tangshan earthquake was judged to be XI on the Mercalli Scale* and 7.8 on the Richter Scale.**

Most powerful earthquake recorded instrumentally
*9.5 Richter Scale***
Southern Chile, 22 May 1960

The earthquake covered a subterranean area of some 620 miles (1000 km) long by 180 miles (290 km) wide. There were a large number of shocks and aftershocks over a wide area.

**Richter Scale – indicates the amount of energy released by the earthquake. There is no upper limit.

Most powerful recorded earthquake in the UK
5.4 Richter Scale**
North Wales, July 1984

Most powerful hurricane recorded instrumentally
Level 5: Catastrophic
Hurricane Andrew, August 1992

Hurricane Andrew was rated 5 (the top level) on the international scale; this is reserved for hurricanes with winds of 155 mph (250 km/h) and storm surges of over 18 ft (5.5 m). The hurricane caused most damage in southern Florida, with gusts of up to 175 mph (282 km/h). Some 33 people died and 80,000 buildings were destroyed. In Dade County, wild animals escaped from a zoo as well as laboratory monkeys infected with the AIDS virus.

Worst storm in Britain
Southern England and West Country, 26–27 November 1703

A vivid, first-hand account of the destruction caused by the storm was written by the author Daniel Defoe. Hurricane force winds of some 73–81 mph (117–130 km/h) battered southern England

and the West Country. The winds caused immense structural damage: at least 400 windmills were destroyed, recorded Defoe, and whole streets of houses were left roofless. Some 123 people died on land, but hundreds more were killed at sea, 1500 alone in Royal Navy ships. Several ships, including warships, were blown right across the Channel to the French coast.

Worst storm in Britain in the 20th century
*Southern and eastern England,
15 October 1987*

Windspeeds rose to hurricane force at 85 mph (137 km/h) and caused considerable structural damage: 19 million trees were destroyed and three million households and businesses were left without electricity. Nineteen people were killed.

Space

Largest planet
Jupiter
85,680 miles (142,800 km) diameter

Jupiter is named after the Roman king of the gods and ruler of the universe. It is composed mainly of hydrogen and helium and its core is thought to be hotter than that of the sun itself, with an estimated temperature of some 5400 °F (3000 °C). Characterized by its vivid, bright red and orange cloud bands, often shot through by massive superbolts of lightning, the atmosphere on rapidly-spinning Jupiter is turbulent and unstable. The Great Red Spot, a colossal, rotating atmospheric storm thousands of miles in diameter, was discovered by the British astronomer, Robert Hooke, in 1664. Jupiter has 16 known moons, the largest of which is Ganymede, discovered by Galileo in 1610, and named after a handsome Trojan prince whom the god Jupiter turned into an eagle and carried off to be a cupbearer to the gods.

Smallest planet
Pluto
1430 miles (2302 km) diameter

Named after the Roman god who ruled over the dead in the Underworld, Pluto is a frozen, lifeless world with an estimated temperature of -382 °F

(-230 °C), thus making it the coldest of the planets. Pluto was only discovered in 1930 by the American astronomer, Clyde Tombaugh, and it follows an eccentric, elongated orbit which crosses that of Neptune. Its one moon, Charon, named after the ferryman who took the dead across the river Styx to Pluto's Underworld, was discovered by James W. Christy in 1978.

Nearest planet
Venus
25,000,000 miles (41,000,000 km) estimated distance from earth

The brightest object in the sky, after the sun and moon, Venus was identified in about 2000 BC by the Babylonians, who associated it with their goddess of love and war, Ishtar. Because of its movements, the planet can be visible both morning and evening, and Venus, named after the Roman goddess of love, was also known as the Shepherd Star, the Morning Star and the Evening Star. Its atmosphere is made up mainly of carbon dioxide and it is the hottest planet with an estimated surface temperature of between 842–896 °F (450–480 °C). Recent discoveries about the surface of Venus have identified vast plains, craters, large but shallow hills and two mountainous regions, named Terra Ishtar and Aphrodite.

Furthest planet visible to the naked eye
Uranus
1,687,000,000 miles (2,720,000,000 km)
estimated distance from earth

Uranus was discovered in 1781 by the British scientist William Herschel, who named it after the Greek god of the sky. Uranus was the first planet to be discovered using a telescope. Its atmosphere is composed of hydrogen, helium and methane, approximately 6215 miles (10,000 km) thick, which makes the planet appear greenish, and it is surrounded by a system of narrow rings. Hurricane-force winds (90–360 mph/145–579 km/h) blow constantly across the planet and Uranus is only marginally less cold than Pluto, with temperatures around -354 °F (-220 °C). Herschel also discovered two of Jupiter's five moons, Titania and Oberon, named after the king and queen of the fairies. Uranus is only visible to the naked eye under certain conditions.

Furthest planet
*Pluto**
3,567,000,000 miles (5,750,000,000 km)
estimated distance from earth

See Smallest planet, p.40.

*Until 1999 Pluto will be closer to the Earth than Neptune because of the unusual shape of its orbit.

Largest star
Σ *Aurigae*
2,336,000,000 miles (3,759,000,000 km) diameter (estimated)

Σ Aurigae is the largest known star to date. A white supergiant, it lies in the constellation of Auriga and is about 2000 light years** away from earth.

Smallest star
Neutron stars (pulsars)
12–19 miles (20–30 km) diameter

Pulsars are tiny, highly-condensed neutron stars which spin at extremely high speeds, and can be very dense, with weights of up to 200 million tons per cubic inch (500 million tonnes per cubic centimetre).

Closest star
Proxima Centauri
*4.22 light years***

Proxima Centauri is a red dwarf, lying in the Centaurus constellation in the Milky Way.

**One light year = 5,874,000,000,000 miles (9,453,000,000,000 km). This is the distance that light travels in one year.

43

Brightest star
Sirius
8.64 light years from earth

Sirius, also known as the Dog Star, is a binary star in the constellation of Canis Major.

Largest asteroid
Ceres
623 miles (1003 km) diameter

Asteroids, also known as minor planets and planetoids, are the small, celestial bodies which move around the sun, mainly between the orbits of Mars and Jupiter (the Asteroid Belt). They appear as tiny points of light in powerful telescopes. Ceres was first discovered in 1801 by Giuseppe Piazzi, a monk who later became Professor of Theology and Professor of Mathematics at Palermo University in Sicily; he named the asteroid after the classical patron goddess of the island. Asteroids of varying sizes frequently fall to earth, causing various degrees of damage. Many scientists believe that the dinosaurs became extinct after a massive asteroid fell to earth, creating huge fires and polluting the air to such an extent that the sun was obliterated for many months, thus destroying vegetation.

First reflecting telescope (reflector)
1668

Invented by Isaac Newton (1643–1727), the reflector works by collecting and focusing light by reflection from a curved mirror (compare refractor below). Light of all colours is reflected in the same way, thus eliminating the blurring and fringing which characterized the early refracting telescopes, such as that used by Galileo. Large mirrors can be constructed more easily than large lenses, can be made more accurate, and can be positioned more easily.

Largest reflector in the world
32 ft 9 in (10 m)
Keck telescope, Mauna Kea Observatory, Hawaii, USA

This multi-mirror telescope was completed in 1992 and is used for optical and infra-red observations. A second Keck telescope is currently being built alongside it. Mauna Kea is a dormant volcano, often snowcapped, and has become the site of a major international astronomical observatory. The viewing conditions here are the finest on earth, the observatory is twice the height of any other observatory and above 40 per cent of the earth's atmosphere.

Largest refracting telescope (refractor)
Lens diameter 40 in (102 cm)
Yerkes Observatory, Williams Bay, Wisconsin, USA

The refractor works by using a large lens (the objective) to gather light rays from a distant source and, by refraction, bending them to a focus. The observer then looks at a magnified image. The main problems include blurring and colour fringing because different colours of light refract by different amounts (eg blue light bends more than red). No-one knows who invented the first refractor, although it may have been Hans Lippershey (died in about 1619), a Dutch spectacle-maker, in around 1608. The Italian scientist, Galileo Galilei (1564–1642) made considerable improvements to the early refractor, constructed several himself and discovered the mountains and craters of the moon, four of Jupiter's moons, and sunspots.

First radio telescope
Circa 1940
USA, invented by Grote Reber

The widespread use of radio in World War I (1914–18) was followed by the rapid expansion of public broadcasting in the 1920s. However, as radio receivers became more sensitive, engineers noticed that increasing amounts of background noise and interference were being picked up. The American company, Bell Telephone Laboratories, commissioned Karl Jansky, a radio engineer, to discover the cause of these problems. Jansky built a receiver/antenna system which worked on short wavelengths. He noticed that underlying the noise caused by thunderstorms and other atmospheric conditions, there was a steady hissing sound. Gradually Jansky realized that this noise came from the centre of our galaxy, Constellation Sagittarius, at the heart of the Milky Way. Having discovered the cause of this 'cosmic static', Jansky's work was complete, but his findings were further developed by amateur astronomer, Grote Reber, from Wheaton, Illinois, who built the first radio telescope. The principles are similar to those of the optical reflecting telescope: a thin sheet of metal covers a paraboloidal surface and radiation is reflected on to a focus; it is collected by an antenna and converted to a voltage.

Largest fully-steerable dish radio telescope
250 ft (76 m)
Jodrell Bank Experimental Station, Cheshire, England

The controversial radio telescope at Jodrell Bank was built largely through the efforts of Sir Bernard

Lovell, supported by Professor Blackett at Manchester University. It was begun in 1952 and completed in 1957, just before the launch of Sputnik I, the first artificial earth satellite. The satellite's carrier rocket was tracked at Jodrell Bank by radar and the installation transmitted the first pictures of the moon's surface sent by the Soviet Luna probe on 6 February 1966.

Largest single-unit radio telescope
1000 ft (305 m) high antenna
Arecibo, Puerto Rico, USA

The installation lies in a hollow lined with wire netting high in the mountains. Information is gathered not through the conventional dish but via an antenna.

Largest radio interferometer (array)
VLA (Very Large Array), Socorro, New Mexico, USA

An interferometer or array works by linking two or more dishes together electronically, thereby effectively making one enormous instrument and greatly increasing capacity. The VLA was completed in 1979 and is laid out in a Y-shape with arms 13 miles (21 km) long. Each arm is a railway, thus allowing the 27 separate telescopes, each with an aperture of 81 ft (25 m), to be moved according to need. The installation gives a very high resolution imaging of cosmic radio sources and is the largest astronomical instrument ever built; it cost over $100 million.

Largest space telescope
Hubble Space Telescope (HST)

The Hubble Space Telescope is a large reflector with a 94 in (2.4 m) primary mirror, a secondary mirror and state-of-the-art instruments that can detect visible, ultraviolet and infra-red light. The telescope was put into orbit on 25 April 1990 about 370 miles (600 km) above the earth by the crew of the space shuttle *Discovery*. Unfortunately there were problems with the reflecting mirror and it became the first satellite to be repaired in space. Hubble, named after Edwin Powell Hubble (1889–1953), one of the twentieth-century's foremost astronomers, is now providing a wealth of data.

First space probe to leave the solar system
Pioneer 10

Unmanned space probes are used for interplanetary study. *Pioneer 10* (launched 1972) was designed to fly past Jupiter and continue out into deep space. Between July 1972 and February 1973, the probe negotiated the asteroid belt and in December 1973 it came to within some 81,000 miles (130,350 km) of Jupiter, sending back over 300 pictures of the planet and its moons, the first space probe to do so. *Pioneer 10* later crossed Neptune's orbit and sent back signals which travelled 2795 million miles (4500 million km), and took four hours to reach earth. *Pioneer 10* passed Pluto in 1986 and in 1987 it was the first manmade object to leave the solar system. It is now billions of miles away and still travelling. The first star it reaches will be Ross 248 in the constellation of Taurus. *Pioneer 10* is now too far away from earth for any further communication, although it is expected to continue transmitting until 2007. It carries a plaque giving details about the earth and its origins.

First man in space
Yuri Alexeyevich Gagarin, USSR

Yuri Gagarin (1934–68) came from Tyuratam and was the son of a carpenter. He volunteered for space training and was launched on 12 April 1961 in *Vostok I*. The duration of the flight was 1 hr 48 min and he travelled some 25,000 miles (40,232 km) at altitudes of between 112 miles (180 km) and

203 miles (327 km) at a speed of approximately 5 miles (8 km) per second. A national hero, Cosmonaut Gagarin was killed in a plane crash while training for another mission.

First woman in space
Valentina Vladimirovna Tereshkova, USSR
On 16 June 1963, Tereshkova (born 1937) was launched into space on the *Vostok 6*. She circled the earth 48 times in 70 hr 50 min, travelling a distance of some 1,225,000 miles (1,971,000 km). She later married the *Vostok 3* pilot, N. Kolayev, and they produced the first 'space baby', Yelena, in 1964.

First man on the moon
Neil A. Armstrong, USA
Neil Armstrong (born 1930), Edward 'Buzz' Aldrin and Michael Collins landed the *Apollo 11* in the Sea of Tranquillity on the moon on 20 July 1969. Armstrong's moon walk was an event unparalleled in human history and his words 'The Eagle has landed' and 'That's one small step for man, one giant leap for mankind' were heard by an estimated 600 million people, about one-fifth of the entire world population.

First Briton in space
Helen Sharman

Sharman, a British chemist, won a competition to travel as a guest on the Russian Mir space station. She flew to Mir on the *Soyuz TM12* craft on 18 May 1991 and returned on 26 May.

Longest space flight for a man
439 days
Valery Polyakov, Russia

Polyakov travelled to the Mir space station on *Soyuz TM18* in January 1994 and returned on *Soyuz TM20* in March 1995. Polyakov has a career total of 680 days in space.

Longest space flight for a woman
174 days
Yelena Kondakova, Russia

Kondakova landed back on earth on 22 March 1995 after 174 days on the Mir space station.

First true spaceship
Columbia Space Shuttle, USA

The *Columbia* Space Shuttle was designed as a reusable craft able to travel between earth and space time and time again. The programme began in January 1972 but it was not until April 1981 that the Shuttle was launched from Cape Canaveral in Florida, after which the craft spent two days in orbit. *Columbia* was designed as a supply ship for a permanently orbiting space station.

First space 'burial'
21 April 1997

A Pegasus rocket was launched from the Canary Islands containing the ashes of over 20 space enthusiasts. Among those who paid over £3000 to orbit the earth for six years were Dr Timothy Leary, famous for his advocacy of an 'alternative', drug-based lifestyle in the 1960s, and Gene Roddenberry, creator of *Star Trek*. The rocket will eventually return to earth and burn up in a flash of light when it re-enters the earth's atmosphere.

The Natural World

Tallest tree

Coast redwood (Sequoia sempervirens)
Max height circa 400 ft (120 m)
Max diameter of trunk 30 ft (10 m)

The coast redwood takes its Latin name from the Cherokee leader Sequoyah, who first developed an alphabet to record the Cherokee language. It is an evergreen tree and grows to immense heights, standing tall and stately. It is native only to the Pacific coast of North America (the 'fog belt'), up to some 3300 ft (1000 m) above sea level. The trees take four to five hundred years to reach maturity, and some individual trees are thought to be over 1500 years old. The wood is soft, fine-grained and easy to work with and these characteristics have led to a serious loss of redwoods through excessive felling. Strict conservation measures are now in force.

Tallest native European tree

Common silver fir (Abies alba)
Approx 165–245 ft (50–75 m) high

The silver fir is native to the mountainous regions of central and southern Europe. However, its attractive lofty stature has made it a popular ornamental tree throughout Europe and it is often found in parks and gardens. The tree demands a moist climate and clean air, so it does not flourish in industrial areas.

Largest tree (girth)

Giant redwood or giant sequoia, also called sierra redwood, big tree, mammoth tree, wellingtonia (Sequoiadendron giganteum)

Max 101 ft 6 in (31 m) circumference at base

The largest-known specimen, the 'General Sherman Tree', is in the Sequoia National Park in the USA. It stands approximately 272 ft (83 m) tall and is estimated to weigh over 6000 tons (6096 tonnes). The trees are native to the western slopes of the Sierra Nevada mountain range in California, and can grow at an altitude of up to 8000 ft (2500 m). This was once thought to be the oldest living species on earth, but recent improvements in dating techniques have shown the samples to be less than 4000 years old. The giant redwood has the thick, spongy bark typical of the species, but its wood is much less easy to work than that of the coast redwood (see opposite, Tallest tree), so it has not been subjected to the same level of exploitation.

Longest-lived tree
Bristlecone pine (Pinus aristata)
Circa 5000 years

The Bristlecone pine is a native of the Rocky Mountains in the south west of North America. It grows extremely slowly in the high altitude conditions, usually over an altitude of 7500 ft (2300 m). It has a gnarled and twisted appearance, with its branches and trunk stripped of bark and bleached white by the sun, and grows to a height of 15–40 ft (5–13 m). Although it appears at first sight to be completely lifeless, the tree is protected from the harsh climate by a high resin content and is very much alive. A specimen at Wheeler Peak, Nevada, is known to be around 4900 years old.

Oldest known surviving species of tree
Maidenhair tree (Ginkgo biloba)

The maidenhair dates from the Mesozoic era, especially the Jurassic period, approximately 160 million years ago, the age of the dinosaurs. The present-day tree is the last representative of the Ginkgoales Order, which originally flourished worldwide but is now found in the wild only in China. The mature maidenhair is a massive tree and some specimens are estimated to be over 1000 years old. It has always been prized for its height (up to 100 ft/30 m) and its beautiful appearance, and is still an intrinsic part of temple gardens in China and Japan. The maidenhair has adapted well to other climates and is now grown all over the world as a decorative, disease-resistant tree, which will tolerate air pollution. In the east, the nut it produces is roasted and eaten as a delicacy – the name, *Ginkgo biloba*, derives from the ancient Chinese or Japanese words for 'silver nut' or 'apricot'. Extracts from the tree are said to have medicinal properties.

Largest seed

Sea coconut or coco de mer (Lodoicea maldivica)

30–40 lb (13–18 kg)

The first Europeans ever to see these enormous seeds were Portuguese explorers, led by Ferdinand Magellan (1480–1521), who found them floating in the sea. The sailors believed them to come from trees rooted in the ocean floor. It was not until 1768 that the first explorers to the Seychelles found the tall, fan palm in deep jungle. The tree was named by Linnaeus after Lodoicea, the most beautiful of King Priam of Troy's daughters. The seed strangely resembles the lower half of a woman's body, both front and back, and for this reason became known as an aphrodisiac. Much prized and valued, the seed was owned only by the rich and powerful. The sea coconut tree is today found on only two islands, Praslin and Curiense; there are only about 4000 trees left and they are strictly protected. The tree grows to about 100–140 ft (30–40 m), has a lovely fan-shaped canopy and lives up to about 800 years.

Smallest seeds

Orchids, such as the tiny, almost microscopic *Platystele stenostachya*, one of the world's smallest flowering plants, produce microscopic seeds. These orchids are native to Central America and the northern parts of South America.

Largest pod
Entada scandens
Approx length 5 ft (1.5 m)

The *Entada* grows in tropical forests and is a woody climber. The pod, though long, is only about 4 in (10 cm) wide; it holds up to 15 seeds and hangs down from the stem (this plant also has one of the longest-known plant stems, up to 460 ft (140 m)). Known in Australia as the Matchbox Bean, the seeds were once used to make matchboxes for wax matches.

Plant with the most massive leaves
Gigantic waterlily (Victoria amazonica)
Up to 6 ft (2 m) diameter

This extraordinary plant was discovered by Thaddeus Haenke in 1801, as he was exploring the Amazon river in Bolivia and Guiana. The huge, flat leaves are turned up at the edges, like a tray, and can support the weight of a child. The weight-bearing, supporting structures under the leaves were copied by the architects who designed one of the glasshouses at Kew Gardens, London.

Smallest plant
Watermeal (Wolffia arrhiza)
0.08 in (2mm) wide

Wolffia is an angiosperm, or flowering plant. Angiosperms are the largest and most diverse group in the plant kingdom and represent approximately 80 per cent of all known green plants now living. This tiny floating herb is scarcely visible to the naked eye.

Largest flower
Rafflesia (Rafflesia arnoldii)
Approx 3 ft 4 in (1 m) diameter, up to 15^1/$_2$ lb (7 kg) weight

The plant was discovered in 1818 by the botanist,

Arnold, who named it after himself. The Rafflesia family is named after Thomas Stamford Raffles, the founder of Singapore. The gigantic bloom is brownish-red with white patches and resembles rotting meat, both in shape and smell, an attribute deliberately intended to attract the insects which are necessary for pollination. The bloom is short-lived; after four days it quickly disintegrates in the tropical heat. Rafflesia is found in tropical forests in Sumatra and Borneo; it grows as a parasite on the roots of other plants and has neither stalk nor leaves.

Largest cactus

Saguaro (Carnegia gigantea)
Up to 53 ft (16 m) height, up to 10 tons (1200 kg) weight

The saguaro is a native of the Sonora Desert, Mexico, and southwest California. It is a striking plant, its thick arms emerging from the stem at the same height on each side, and turning upwards, resembling a candelabra. It can store up to 5280 pints (3000 litres) of water and lives up to 200 years.

Largest mushroom

Puffball (Calvatia gigantea)
Up to 5 ft (1.55 m) diameter

This huge specimen was found in the USA, although puffballs are generally much smaller, averaging around 9 in–1 ft (0.2–0.3 m) in diameter. A puffball contains around three trillion spores which it sheds when it bursts. Puffballs are also found in Europe, where certain varieties can be eaten. They also come in useful in an emergency – a mature puffball, full of spores, is very absorbent and can stop bleeding in humans.

Heaviest mushroom
Stone fungus (Polyphorus mylittae)
Up to 80 lb (36 kg)

This curious fungus has the appearance of a large stone and although it grows underground it is a mushroom, not a true truffle. Its white flesh can be roasted and eaten – in Australia it is known as 'Blackfellow's bread'.

Most poisonous mushroom
Death cap (Amanita phalloides)
Mortality rate 60-100 per cent

Death cap can easily be mistaken for an edible mushroom of similar appearance and does not taste bad. Symptoms only appear 9–14 hours after eating, by which time it is usually too late. The chemicals in death cap dissolve blood corpuscles.

Only plant which can change its shape
Rose of Jericho or resurrection plant
(Anastatica hierochuntica)

This curious plant responds to the prevailing climatic conditions by changing its shape. When there is enough moisture, its branches spread out in a star shape and small, white flowers bloom. In dry conditions, the branches turn in, forming a ball which protects the fruit within. Rose of Jericho is easily uprooted and it bowls along in the wind across the desert sands, often startling people and animals as it suddenly appears apparently out of nowhere. As soon as it reaches moist conditions, the plant opens out and resumes its former shape. Rose of Jericho is also known as Mary's flower and was often taken home from the Holy Land by pilgrims.

Longest herbivorous dinosaur
Diplodocus
Up to 85 ft (26 m) long

Sauropods were active in the Jurassic period some 135–200 million years ago. These are the longest land animals ever to have lived and include the *Barapasaurus* (49 ft/15 m), *Cetiosaurus* (60 ft/ 183 m), *Brachiosaurus* (75 ft/23 m) and the longest of them all, *Diplodocus*. These gigantic, long-necked, four-legged creatures survived for some 50 million years. In 1986, huge bones were discovered in New Mexico, USA, suggesting an even longer creature, possibly up to 100 ft (30 m) long. The skeleton was incomplete, however, although this 'new' dinosaur has provisionally been given the name *Seismosaurus* ('earthquake lizard').

Largest herbivorous dinosaur

Brachiosaurus
75 ft (23 m) long, 21 ft (6.4 m) shoulder height, 90 tons (91 tonnes) weight

Brachiosaurus lived in the late Jurassic period, 135–200 million years ago. A complete skeleton has shown it to be the most massive, although not the longest, animal ever to have walked the earth (see above, Longest herbivorous dinosaur). It was more than ten times the weight of the modern African elephant (see Largest land mammal, p.68). Recent discoveries in Tanzania suggest that it could have been even larger than present estimates.

Largest carnivorous dinosaur

Tyrannosaurus
Up to 49 ft (15 m) long, 18 ft (5.3 m) tall, 8 tons (8.13 tonnes) weight

The *Tyrannosaurus* ('tyrant lizard') is the largest terrestrial carnivore yet known. Its supremacy came in the late Cretaceous Period 65-135 million years ago. The head alone was over 4 ft (1.25 m) long and the teeth were up to 6 in (15 cm) long. *Tyrannosaurus* walked upright, horizontally to the ground, and was capable of short bursts of high-speed running on its powerful hind legs. The front legs were small and useless for weight-bearing. The *Tyrannosaurus* is thought to have been one of the most highly-evolved and successful of the dinosaurs.

Smallest carnivorous dinosaur
Compsognathus
2 ft (60 cm) long 8 lb (3.6 kg) weight

The little *Compsognathus* ('pretty jaw'), was a two-legged creature, about the size of a modern chicken. It could run very fast and had a long neck and tail. Active in the late Jurassic period (135–200 million years ago), *Compsognathus* was similar to the first known bird, *Archaeopteryx* (see opposite).

First flying reptiles
Eudimorphodon, Pterodactylus

The first flying reptiles (pterosaurs) appeared in the Late Triassic period and spanned the Jurassic period until the early Cretaceous period (approximately 130–260 million years ago). The early

Eudimorphodon had a $2^1/_2$ in (6.25 cm) wingspan and its featherless wings consisted of membraneous flaps of skin extending from the elongated fourth digits of each foreleg and rejoining the body at the upper leg. More familiar, perhaps, is the *Pterodactylus* which had a similar structure, but a longer tail and shorter neck than the *Eudimorphodon*. The largest known (incomplete) skeleton, *Quetzalcoatlus*, suggests that flying reptiles could weigh as much as 143 lb (65 kg) and have a wingspan of 39 ft (12 m). If this is so, then they would be the largest flying vertebrates ever to have existed on the earth.

First bird
Archaeopteryx lithographica

An almost complete skeleton of *Archaeopteryx*, together with a single feather and an impression of its plumage, was found in southern Germany and indicated that the bird was about 14 in (35 cm) long. Its first appearance is thought to have come in the Jurassic period (135–200 million years ago). The skeleton indicates a small head with large eyes and sharp teeth, and a long bony tail. It had clawed feet and three clawed digits on each wing. Most palaeontologists agree that *Archaeopteryx* was insectivorous, gliding from tree to tree and using its sharp claws to climb up tree trunks and along branches in order to launch itself into the air. It was almost certainly warm-blooded and represents a vital link between reptiles and birds.

Largest mammal
Blue whale (Balaenoptera musculus)
80–90 ft (24–27 m) long, 128–148 tons (130–150 tonnes) weight

The blue whale is also called Sibbald's rorqual and sulphur bottom (because of the coating of yellowish, microscopic plants which sometimes grow on its underside). Blue whales are a dark, blue-grey colour with paler markings, and usually travel alone or in pairs, rarely in schools. They live in deep waters both north and south of the equator and feed on krill (tiny, shrimp-like creatures). Blue whales have extremely large lungs (which may weigh more than 1 ton (1.016 tonnes), can dive as deep as 1500 ft (450 m) and stay submerged for up to two hours. Intensive whaling in the past decimated the whale numbers and very large specimens are rarely seen today.

Largest land mammal
African elephant (Loxodonta africana africana)
Approx 10 ft (3 m) height, 6 tons (6.096 tonnes) weight, 27 ft (9 m) long

Male African elephants rarely grow to heights of more than 11 ft (3.5 m), although a specimen was found to be 12 ft (3.6 m) at the shoulder. Elephants are herbivores and their weight varies according to the season and what vegetation is available. The elephant's massive legs are specially designed to bear the huge weight of its body. The limb bones are heavy and solid, and have no marrow; the soles of the feet are made of soft and horny layers and have a fatty cushion which helps to spread weight evenly. The feet can be up to 20 in (50 cm) across. Elephants can neither run nor jump, but they can make good speed over short distances. The tusks are really the elephant's upper incisor teeth and, like teeth, are composed of dentine with an enamel cap. The average male has tusks with a paired weight of some 121 lb (55 kg). One of the heaviest tusks ever found was 235 lb (107 kg). Newborn calves stand about 3 ft (0.9 m) tall and weigh some 200 lb (90 kg).

Heaviest land mammal
See Largest land mammal opposite.

Tallest mammal
Giraffe (Giraffa camelopardalis)
18 ft (5.5 m), male, average height

Giraffes are found only in Africa today, but in prehistoric times they lived in both Europe and Asia. A relation of the okapi, the giraffe lives in the dry lands and open wooded areas south of the Sahara desert. It feeds mainly on leaves and, because of its elongated neck, is superbly equipped to reach the topmost branches of the trees. Its long, black, prehensile tongue curls around the leaves and its thick lips are not easily damaged by thorns. On the other hand, the giraffe cannot bend easily and it must straddle its legs to drink, although it can survive for long periods without water. Giraffes are almost constantly awake (they need only about one hour's sleep a day), and move about in herds. Their only predators are humans and lions – and a single lion can rarely kill a giraffe which will defend itself vigorously with its powerful kick. The young are born after 14 and a half months gestation and are about 6 ft (2 m) high, with a weight of some 130 lb (59 kg).

Smallest mammal
Kitti's hog-nosed bat (Craseonycteris thonglongyai)
6 in (15 cm) wingspan, 1^1/$_2$ in (4 cm) body length

This tiny creature weighs only 0.42–0.84 oz (1.5–3 g) and is found in small groups in bamboo forests and teak plantations, where it was first discovered and documented in 1974. A nocturnal animal, it is insectivorous and spends the daylight hours roosting in caves. The young are born live, have fur and are suckled by the female. Kitti's hog-nosed bat (also called the butterfly bat) is in serious danger of becoming extinct as the total world population is only about 200 individuals.

Fastest land mammal (short distances)
Cheetah (Acinonyx jubatus)
71 mph (105 km/h) (max)

Cheetahs live in open grasslands and semi-arid deserts in Africa and southwest Asia. They hunt small-hoofed animals, such as impala and gazelle, which gather in herds out in the open, away from cover. To be successful, therefore, the cheetah needs to be able to attack animals moving at speed away from it. The cheetah can reach 0-50 mph (0-80 km/h) within 2 seconds and a maximum speed of 71 mph (105 km/h). The average chase covers about 600 ft (183 m) and lasts 20 seconds, before the prey is killed swiftly and cleanly with a bite through the neck. However, the cheetah may have spent many hours watching and stalking its potential prey and, even so, only about half of its chases end in a kill.

Fastest land mammal (long distances)

Pronghorn antelope (Antilocapra americana)

45 mph (70 km/h) over 4 miles (6.4 km)

The pronghorn antelope lives in the open grass and bushlands of the western USA, Canada and parts of Mexico. It has a heavy, thickset body with long, slim legs. The black horns are shed and regrown annually. The pronghorn, with its ability to run as fast as 55 mph (86 km/h) over short distances as well as maintain a steady 45 mph (70 km/h) over longer distances, proved to be an enjoyable challenge for hunters, whose activities almost brought the animal to extinction. The pronghorn antelope, now protected, has increased in number to about 500,000 animals.

Slowest mammal

Three-toed sloth (Bradypus tridactylus)

6–8 ft (1.8–2.5 m) per min (average ground speed)

The sloth lives in the rainforests of Central and South America. Often despised for its apparent laziness and lack of aesthetic appeal (a 16th-century Spanish explorer noted that he had never seen 'an uglier or more useless creature'), the sloth is, nevertheless, superbly adapted to its habitat.

Although it is nearly helpless when on the ground, where it must haul itself along by its front legs, the sloth is much more nimble up in the trees where it lives most of the time. Its complex stomach digests food (mainly leaves) for about a month, and faeces and urine are passed only once a week. It has very low metabolic rates for its body weight of some 7.7–9.4 lb (3.5–4.5 kg) and it spends much of its time hanging upside down from branches. Its coat, which is never groomed, often acquires a greenish colour from the algae growing on it, and the hair grows in the opposite direction from that of most animals, ie from stomach to back, thereby preventing waterlogging when the animal is hanging upside down. The quiet, slow-moving, arboreal life of the sloth has ensured that it remains almost unnoticeable to predators in the dense forests, and it has few competitors for the food it needs. The continuing survival of this unique animal depends on humans and their willingness to protect the remaining tropical forests.

Longest-lived mammal (marine)

Humpback whale (Megaptera novaeangliae) and Fin whale (Balaenoptera physalus)
Both species can live up to 95 years

Longest-lived mammal (land)
Asiatic elephant (Elephas maximus)
Up to 60 years (80 in captivity)

In the wild, elephants live in close-knit groups, governed by complex social patterns of behaviour. The family unit is led by the oldest female, the matriarch. If she is older than 50, she will no longer be capable of reproduction, but she continues to guide her family, using her long experience to ensure the group's survival.

Mammal which lives at greatest altitude
Mount Everest pika (Ochotona wollastoni)
Up to 20,000 ft (6100 m) altitude

There are 12 species of pika, a small, short-eared, tailless animal, similar to a rabbit. Pikas are adapted to a variety of habitats and can live on rocky slopes and in mountainous areas, as well as on open plains and semi-deserts, where they spend much of their time underground. Pikas are widespread throughout North America, eastern Europe, the Middle East and parts of Asia. Brownish-grey in colour, the pika grows up to about 8 in (20 cm) long and weighs up to about

10 oz (280 g). Pikas eat most kinds of vegetation in
their habitat and do not hibernate.

Mammal which lives at greatest depth
Myotis lucifugus
Up to 3000 ft (915 m) depth

Myotis lucifugus is a species of bat, some of which
inhabit very deep caves and can survive
temperatures as low as 23 °F (-5 °C) for core body
temperature when hibernating. There are about
1000 species of bat worldwide and they are found
in most parts of the world. Bats congregate in caves
for roosting and hibernating because of the stable
temperatures and the fact that they will be
undisturbed. Sometimes they form vast groups
(one cave in Texas was estimated to contain 20
million bats). The floor of the caves often becomes
thick with bat droppings (guano) which is collected
and used for fertilizer and, in the past, was used in
gunpowder. There are many myths and legends
about bats and they engender considerable
apprehension in some people, perhaps because of
the erroneous fear that the bats will become
entangled in their hair. It may also be because,
being primarily nocturnal, bats are seen as
'creatures of the night'. All bat species found in the
UK are now protected.

Deepest-diving mammal
Sperm whale (Physeter catodon)
Up to 10,000 ft (3050 m) depth

Sperm whales can stay underwater for up to two hours, although marine biologists are not altogether certain why they do so – it may be that they are hunting for giant squid. The sperm whale is very distinctive in shape, characterized by a large, squarish head which makes up a third of its length. In the past, the sperm whale was hunted extensively for its oil, used for candles and cosmetics, and for ambergris, a substance formed in the whale's intestine and used as a fixer for perfumes. Sperm whales often form large schools of up to several hundred individuals. The most famous fictional whale, Moby Dick, in the novel of the same name by Herman Melville, was a white sperm whale.

Largest primate
Gorilla (Gorilla gorilla)
Up to 6 ft 6 in (2 m) high, 310–400 lb (140–180 kg) adult male

The gorilla has a fearsome reputation, perhaps because of its powerful, muscular body, but in fact it is a gentle animal, living in close-knit family groups in the equatorial forests of Africa. The unit is led by an older male, who is distinguished by the silvery hair on his back, and there will be from five to 40 individuals in the group. Gorillas are herbivorous and move each day to find fresh food. They are generally shy animals and will only become ferocious when provoked. Together with the chimpanzee, the gorilla is man's closest relative. In the wild, gorillas live about 28 years, longer in captivity.

Smallest primate
Lesser mouse lemur (Microcebus myoxinus)
Up to 4 in (12.5 cm) body length, 5–6 in (13–15 cm) tail length

Lemurs are found only on the island of Madagascar, off the east coast of Africa, and appear to have evolved after the island broke away from the mainland millions of years ago. The lesser mouse lemur has large eyes, a long, bushy tail and slender limbs. Mainly nocturnal and arboreal, this lemur eats insects, small mammals and fruit. There are some 15 species of lemur, of which the ring-tailed is the best known. Recent reports indicate that a previously unknown species, even smaller than the lesser mouse lemur, has been discovered on the island.

Longest gestation period (mammal)
Indian elephant (Elephas maximus)
20–22 months (average)

The Indian elephant gives birth to one calf which is suckled for at least four and sometimes six years.

Shortest gestation period (mammal)
Virginia (Common) opossum (Didelphis virginiana)
13 days

The young Virginia opossum weighs only 2^1/$_2$ oz (70 g) at birth. Opossums are marsupials (animals whose young start development in the womb, but are born in an immature state and complete their development in the marsupium or 'pouch'). Virginia opossums are found in the USA and Canada, and can survive in a wide range of habitats, such as forests, grasslands and mountains. They have a grey/black coat, pointed snout and a long, prehensile tail. Nocturnal and omnivorous, the Virginia opossum often feigns death when attacked, giving rise to the expression 'playing possum'.

Longest hibernation
Hoary marmot (Marmota caligata)
Up to 9 months

Marmots are rodents (they have strong teeth for gnawing), are herbivorous and related to squirrels, but are heavier and more powerful. There are 15 species, distributed in North America, Central Asia and Europe. Marmots live in close-knit family groups in a system of deep, interconnecting burrows. Generally round in shape, with brownish fur, marmots grow to a length of 11–23 in (30–60 cm), have short, bushy tails and short legs. Depending on the prevailing climate and temperatures, hoary marmots may hibernate for up to 9 months. They collect together in the burrow and the last one in makes a 'plug' for the access hole. Survival depends on utilizing stored fat reserves and, in spite of their very low metabolic rate while dormant, they will have lost at least one quarter of their bodyweight when they wake up. Marmots are hunted for their flesh and fur.

Largest horse
Clydesdale
Up to 18 hands* high

Local draught horses in Lanarkshire, Scotland, were crossbred with Flemish horses to produce the Clydesdale, which dates from the 18th century. The breed was used extensively in agricultural and timber work and also to haul coal from the local mines. Today it is used mainly on ceremonial occasions to pull brewers' drays, and as a drum horse in military parades. The shire is the result of crossing the Old English black horse with medieval chargers, and was used for hundreds of years as a basic carthorse. Despite their size, shires are gentle and willing.

Smallest horse
Falabella
Up to 7 hands* high

Falabellas were developed by the Falabella family in Argentina, and are partly derived from the Shetland pony. They are strong for their height and gentle in temperament. Falabellas are kept as pets and, although they are occasionally used as miniature carriage horses, they are not ridden.

Largest dog
Height: Irish wolfhound 28–35 in (71–90 cm)
Weight: Mastiff 190–220 lb (86–100 kg)

The Irish wolfhound was probably introduced to Ireland by the Romans and the Irish chieftains soon took to them. They were used in hunting and for protection. The mastiff is slightly heavier than the St Bernard and was developed by the Romans as a

*A hand is 4 in (10 cm)

fighting dog. In Britain, mastiffs were kept as watchdogs, especially in country areas. Despite their fearsome size and appearance, mastiffs are good-natured and very courageous.

Smallest dog

Chihuahua
Order 6–9 in (15–23 cm) high, 2–6 lb (1–3 kg)
weight

The Chihuahua takes its name from the Mexican state from where it was first exported to the USA. It is even-tempered and friendly, but its fragile frame means it needs careful handling. The Pekingese grows to about the same height as the Chihuahua, but is more robust and weighs around 7–12 lb (3–6 kg).

Largest cat

Maine Coon, Ragdoll
Up to 20 lb (9.1 kg)

The Maine coon is the oldest indigenous breed in the USA. Its origins are, however, obscure: it is said that the breed arrived with the Vikings from Scandinavia and also that the cat is the result of crossbreeding between domestic cats and raccoons. Maine coons are powerfully built and muscular, and grow thick winter coats. The ragdoll is so-called because of its curious habit of becoming completely relaxed when being stroked or picked up. A comparatively recent breed, ragdolls are strong and robustly built with thick, silky fur and blue eyes.

Smallest cat
Singapura
6 lb (2.7 kg)

The Singapura was developed in the USA in the 1970s from the feral (half wild) cats of Singapore which live in the streets and are known locally as 'drain cats'. Singapuras are attractively coloured, cream or ivory, with bronze markings and have almond-shaped eyes. They are very rare and thus are extremely valuable.

Tallest flightless bird
Ostrich (Struthio camelus)
Up to 8 ft (2.5 m) high (male)

The ostrich lives in the dry plains of East Africa and is omnivorous, eating mainly plants, fruits, seeds, leaves and shoots, although it will also take small animals such as lizards. Its long neck is pink and featherless, as are its legs, which contrast with the graceful black and white wing and tail plumage, much sought-after in Victorian times when it was used to decorate ladies' hats. Ostriches, by virtue of their height, make good sentries and they often graze with herds of animals such as zebra and gnu, acting as early-warning lookouts. In return, the grazing animals disturb seeds and nuts for the ostriches. Ostriches are kept in farms in South Africa and are bred mainly for their skins, plumage and, to a lesser extent, for meat.

Tallest flying bird
Siberian crane (Grus leucogeranus)
Up to 5 ft (1.5 m) tall

Cranes are found all over the world, on every continent except South America and Antarctica. There are 15 known species and there is evidence that these tall, elegant birds have existed since the Pliocene period, some 2 million years ago. Cranes are most often found in open country, usually near water – marshes, lakes and the seashore. They eat fish, small animals, roots and fruits and can live to a great age. Although shy birds, they are very gregarious and migrate in large flocks. Several species have a particularly striking habit of 'dancing', which includes bobbing and bowing and jumping up with open wings; some even throw a stick in the air and catch it as it falls. Such displays have formed models for African tribal dances. The

Whopping Crane is one of the world's rarest birds, and at least four other species are threatened with extinction.

Smallest bird
Bee hummingbird (Mellisuga helenae)
2 in (5cm)

The bee hummingbird of Cuba is smaller than some insects and weighs less than 0.07 oz (2 g). Hummingbirds are highly-specialized birds, living in the forests and open country of the Americas, often at high altitudes, and feeding on nectar, which they draw from flowers through their long fine bills, and small insects. The tongue is also long and fine and it rolls inwards at the edges to form a kind of tube which allows the bird to draw up and swallow the nectar. Since there is nowhere for the bird to perch while feeding, it hovers close to the flower, beating its wings very fast to hold its position. Hummingbirds are the only birds which can fly backwards, and they move solely by flying – their short legs and small feet mean that they are unable to walk at all. There are over 300 species of hummingbird, many with brightly-coloured, iridescent green and blue plumage – quite unlike the more sober black and white swifts of Europe, to which they are related.

Heaviest flying bird
Kori (giant) bustard (Ardeotis kori)
Up to 54 in (134 cm) long, up to 35 lb (16 kg) weight

The kori bustard resembles an ostrich or crane in appearance, and lives in dry open country in east and south Africa, feeding on buds, leaves, seeds and insects. Its weight brings it near to the physical limits for flying and it flies only reluctantly and for short distances. On the other hand, it can run fast to escape predators.

Largest wingspan
Wandering albatross (Diomeda exulans)
Over 11 ft 6 in (3.5 m) wingspan

There are some 14 species of albatross, all large, long-winged, gliding seabirds, which feed on most kinds of sea animal found near the surface of the water. The wandering albatross spends much of its time, when not breeding, in the air. Its characteristic gliding motion depends on air speeds and currents and its wings have the highest aspect ratio (proportion of length to breadth) of any bird, from 20–25. The albatross makes use of the different windspeeds at sea level and higher – it flies up to around 50 ft (15 m) above sea level – and can travel many miles without beating its wings.

The wandering albatross has suffered very much at the hands of humans; the bird often follows ships and, in the past, sailors regarded it as a bad omen, bringing high winds and dangerous seas – this superstition may have arisen because high winds meant good flying conditions to the albatross – and killed the birds at every opportunity, selling them for meat and for their plumage. In addition, the fighting in the Pacific during World War II (1939–45) devastated some breeding colonies. Wandering albatrosses raise only one chick every two years so their numbers fall drastically if breeding is interrupted.

Fastest-flying bird (non-diving speed)
Swifts
Up to 105 mph (170 km/h)

Swifts are the most aerial of birds, some even mating and passing the night on the wing. Their bodies are specially adapted for high-speed flying, with streamlined shape and short legs – although this means that the bird has great difficulty in launching itself off the ground if it should fall. The head is small, with a short beak and very wide mouth. There are 68 species of swift and they are found all over the world except in polar regions, New Zealand, most of Australia and some tropical islands.

Fastest-flying bird (diving speed)
Peregrine falcon (Falco peregrinus)
100–275 mph (160–440 km/h)

These figures are estimated speeds of a peregrine falcon's gravity-assisted dive or stoop (that is, the dive which the bird makes to catch its prey on the wing). Peregrine falcons are found on all continents except Antarctica. They live in various habitats, mainly in mountainous areas or by seacliffs, although some live in forests, and feed almost exclusively on other birds, especially wild duck, which they catch in flight, grasping with their powerful talons. Peregrine falcons are thought to mate for life and they return to the same spot each year to breed. The proud bearing and striking appearance of the peregrine has ensured it a prominent place in falconry for hundreds of years.

Fastest wing beat
Hummingbirds
Up to 90 beats per second

Small hummingbirds, such as the vervain hummingbird, attain these speeds while hovering to gather nectar from a flower (see above, Smallest bird). It is said that even faster speeds (up to 200 beats a second) are attained during mating displays.

Highest-flying bird
Ruppell's vulture (Gyps rueppellii)

No accurate measurements can be given for the height that these birds can attain, although individuals have been known to fly as high as an aeroplane. There are seven *Gyps* species, all gregarious, carrion-feeding birds living in open or mountainous terrain in hot countries in Africa, Asia and Europe. Like other vultures they have large bodies, featherless heads and necks and powerful wings, which are specially adapted for gliding. The birds soar to great heights, using air currents, then glide in immense circles looking for dead or dying animals on the ground, aided by their amazing eyesight – they can spot a carcase from several thousand feet up. Then they plummet like a stone to the ground and rush to the food with outstretched wings and neck. Vultures have always been despised for their role as scavengers of dead meat, but in fact they perform a useful service, clearing up matter which could harbour disease if left to rot. Vultures are well-equipped for their lifestyle – the hooked beak, for example, is designed for dismembering and tearing at flesh, and their stomachs secrete powerful enzymes which break down bones. The featherless heads and necks can more easily be kept clean while feeding, whereas feathers would quickly become matted with blood and unhygienic.

Fastest-swimming bird

Emperor penguin (Aptenodytes forsteri)
10 knots (11 mph/20 km/h) (double these
speeds for short bursts)

The flightless penguin is the most marine of birds; it can swim as fast as a seal and has webbed toes and wings that cannot be folded. The emperor penguin is the largest species and can grow up to 4 ft (120 cm) high. Emperors inhabit the Antarctic where they live on crustaceans, such as krill, fish and squid. Emperor penguins are very gregarious and often live closely packed together in huge colonies, also known as rookeries. They nest on the ground, holding the single egg on their feet for warmth, and rear only one or two chicks each year. Like other species, the emperor penguin is threatened by pollution and depletion of its food resources through commercial fishing.

Deepest-diving bird

Emperor penguin (Aptenodytes forsteri)
880 ft (268 m)

This dive was measured by a depth recorder attached to the bird. The penguin shape is specially adapted for swimming – its streamlined shape complemented by dense, completely waterproof plumage which retains body heat. See also Fastest-swimming bird, p.89.

Largest bird's nest
Mallee fowl (Leipoa ocellata)
5 ft (1.5 m) high, 16 ft (5 m) diameter (above ground)

The male mallee fowl of southern Australia spends almost its entire life occupied with building and maintaining its nest. It first excavates a hole in the ground about 3 ft (1 m) deep and 10–13 ft (3–4 m) in diameter, containing an egg chamber. It then fills and covers this with a mound of decaying vegetable matter. The female lays the eggs (15–24) and the fermenting vegetable matter helps to keep them warm. The male maintains a constant check on the temperature of the nest by thrusting its bill into the mound: if it's too cold, the bird piles on more insulation; if too hot, it opens up the mound to let air in. In contrast to its vigilant preoccupation with the nest, the mallee fowl leaves the chicks entirely to fend for themselves. After hatching, they struggle up through the mound and arrive in the world in a weak and vulnerable condition. They receive neither food nor protection from either parent, but can fly within 24 hours of surfacing. Mallee fowl are quiet, shy birds and feed on seeds, buds and some insects.

Smallest bird's nest
Hummingbirds

The smallest hummingbirds, such as the tiny bee hummingbird (see Smallest bird, p.84), build minute, cup-shaped nests made from animal down, mosses and lichens held together with spider silk and saliva. They are attached to twigs, vines and the roofs of caves by plant fibres and usually contain two eggs.

Largest bird's egg
Ostrich (Struthio camelus)
6 in (15 cm) long, 5 in (13 cm) diameter, 3 lb (1.4 kg) weight

Ostriches lay their eggs in shallow pits in sandy soil about 3 ft (1 m) across. The pit is excavated by the male who also looks after the eggs and protects the chicks when they hatch. See also Tallest flightless bird, p.82. The largest egg in proportion to body weight is that of the kiwi, whose egg may be up to 25 per cent of the female's body weight when laid.

Smallest bird's egg
Bee hummingbird (Mellisuga helenae)
0.3 in (7.5 mm) long

The eggs can weigh less than 0.02 oz (0.5 g) and

take 12–19 days to hatch. See also Smallest bird, Smallest bird's nest, pp.84, 91.

Largest fish
Whale shark (Rhincodon typus)
Up to 50 ft (15 m) long

Despite its terrifying appearance, the whale shark is docile and harmless to man; in fact divers sometimes swim beside them, holding on to their dorsal fins, without danger. The whale shark lives in warm seas such as the Atlantic, Pacific and Indian Oceans, feeding on small planktonic animals which it ingests by filtering through a grille as it glides through the water. The whale shark usually grows to about 45 ft (13.5 m) but specimens up to 50 ft (15 m) have been found.

Smallest fish
Pygmy goby (Pandaka pygmaea)
Approx 1/2 in (1.2 cm)

The pygmy goby is a freshwater fish from the Philippines and is the smallest known vertebrate (animal with a backbone) in the world.

Fish living at greatest depth
Brotulids
Up to 24,000 ft (7300 m) deep

There are some 200 species of brotulid, primitive fish which live in the deepest seas. In general, they have elongated pointed tails, a single long, spineless fin and range from a few inches or centimetres to 3 ft (90 cm) in length. They inhabit only deep waters and undersea caves, where there is little if any light and, consequently, many brotulids are sightless.

Fastest fish
Sailfish (Istiophorus albicans)
Up to 60 mph (110 km/h)

It is difficult for biologists to measure speeds of swimming fish accurately, but the sailfish is certainly among the fastest. It is a large fish, some 11 ft (3.5 m) long and weighs about 120 lb (55 kg). It has powerful muscles and an extended and enlarged dorsal fin which forms a sail shape, hence its name. Sailfish frequent tropical Atlantic waters and the Gulf Stream off the American coast, where they are regarded by fishermen as a particular challenge – they can put up a tremendous fight for a long time when caught on a line.

Most poisonous fish
Weever fish (Trachinus draco), stonefish (Synaceia horrida)

Found in the Mediterranean Sea, the deadly weever fish carries a toxic cocktail in its opercula (bony flaps covering the gill slits) and dorsal fin which, if touched, can kill human beings. The chemistry of the poison is not yet known and there is no antidote. Victims suffer instant, stabbing pain which becomes agonizing; nausea, delirium, breathing difficulties, convulsions and loss of consciousness may follow, ending in death. The stonefish is found in shallow, tropical waters in the Indian and Pacific oceans. The average stonefish is about 12 in (30 cm) long and resembles a piece of rock on the ocean floor. If approached it will lie perfectly still, blending in with its surroundings, and is thus difficult to see. The dorsal spines of the stonefish have bulbous poison-filled glands at their bases, which the fish can eject when threatened. This powerful neurotoxin (nerve poison) can be fatal to humans, and is known to have killed bathers who have accidentally trodden on stonefish in the shallow waters off northern Australia.

Largest jellyfish
Arctic giant (Cyanea arctica)
Up to 90 in (2.28 m) bell diameter, 120 ft (36.5 m) tentacles

The Arctic giant is the longest animal in the world. It lives in the northeast Atlantic and swims by rhythmically pulsating the bell. The tentacles and bell are covered with stinging cells which paralyze the prey trapped by the tentacles.

Most poisonous jellyfish
Seawasps (Chironex and Chiropsalmus)

Seawasps live in the Indian Ocean between Australia and Malaysia, and are also found in shallow waters off the Pacific coast of Queensland, Australia. Their venom can kill a human within three minutes.

Most poisonous mollusc
Spotted octopus (Octopus maculosus)

The spotted octopus lives in the Indo-Pacific and Indian Oceans and produces a powerful cephalotoxin, a neuromuscular poison, which causes stinging pain, numbness in the mouth and neck, blurring of the vision, paralysis, coma and, usually, death. Octopuses always have eight arms and vary in size from about 2 in (5 cm) to 18 ft (5.4 m), with an armspan of almost 30 ft (9 m). The eight arms have fleshy suckers that enable the animal to hold its prey with considerable power. Most octopuses move by crawling along the sea bottom, using the suckers, but if alarmed they can eject a spurt of water which propels them quickly backwards, away from danger. They can also eject an inky substance which spreads through the water and acts as a screen while the octopus escapes.

Largest toad
Cane toad (Bufo marinus)
Up to 9 in (23 cm) long, 1 lb (450 g) weight

The cane toad is also called the marine, giant and Mexican toad. The genus *Bufo* is found all over the world, except in Antarctica, Madagascar and Polynesia. In the 1930s, Australian sugar cane growers imported 100 adult cane toads following enthusiastic reports from sugar growers in Central and South America that it had destroyed large quantities of pests which prey on the sugarcane. The cane toads in Australia were allowed complete freedom to spread and breed and, because they are not native to the country, they had no natural enemies to keep numbers down. In addition, the species breeds all year round and the inevitable result was that they soon reached plague proportions. It also became apparent that the toads were eating as many useful and beneficial creatures (including Australia's native frogs) as harmful and destructive creatures. If threatened, the cane toad produces noxious secretions on its skin and can squirt poison from glands behind its eyes up to 3 ft (1 m) away. These poisons have been known to kill dogs, and even in adults can cause temporary paralysis. Possibly the only beneficial result of the disastrous decision to import the cane toad into Australia (which was taken against advice from biologists) is that there is a ready supply of toads for use in research and teaching, and there is some commercial demand for the skins, which are tanned and used as leather.

Largest toad in UK
Common toad (Bufo bufo)
Up to 6 in (15 cm)

The common toad has a compact body and short legs; it can both walk and hop. Its skin is thick, dry and warty – not slimy – and it has poison glands behind its eyes and in the warts on its back, although these pose no threat to humans. There are only two species of toad in the UK, the other is the natterjack (*Bufo calamita*).

Largest frog
Goliath frog (Conraua goliath)
Up to 1 ft (30 cm) long, $7^1/_4$ lb (3.3 kg) weight

The Goliath frog is also known as the West African giant frog or *Gigantorana goliath*.

Smallest frog
Brazilian brachycephalids
$^1/_2$ in (10 mm) long

Most poisonous frog
Koikoi (poison-arrow frog) (Phyllobates bicolor)

The poison-arrow frog is a native of the rainforests of Colombia, South America. Its poison is deadly; it is estimated that 0.0000004 oz (0.00001 g) can kill a human. The Choco Indians have long used the frogs to provide poison for their arrows – one tiny frog can secrete enough poison from its skin for 50 arrows. Poisonous frogs are often very brightly coloured to warn predators to keep away.

Longest snake
Reticulated python (Python reticulata)
Up to 33 ft (10 m) long

The reticulated python lives in the humid rainforests and bushy scrublands of southeast Asia. It is heavy as well as long and weighs some 220 lb (100 kg). The python feeds on birds and mammals and can kill animals as large as pigs and small deer – even children and small adults have been cited as its victims. The reticulated python does not bite, but coils itself around the prey and squeezes it with its immensely powerful muscles until the animal is suffocated. After a large meal, the snake lies absolutely still for several days, eventually disgorging a ball of fur, feathers or hair. Its stomach can expand until quite distended to accommodate the prey – which is swallowed whole – and the snake can quickly regurgitate the entire contents of its stomach if it is threatened by danger and needs to move quickly.

Fastest snake
Black mamba (Dendroaspis polylepis)
up to 7 mph (11 km/h), short bursts over level ground

Mambas are tree-dwelling snakes of central and southern Africa, although the black mamba tends to spend more time on the ground than other mamba species. The snake grows to about 14 ft (4.5 m) long and is very poisonous; the venom can kill a human within ten minutes. Black mambas attack with great ferocity and rush with unbelievable speed on their victims, which have little chance of escape. The fangs at the front of the nose (maxilla) are designed like a hypodermic syringe, injecting the venom into the prey with great force. A large black mamba can secrete enough venom to kill up to 10 people. The poison affects the heart and nervous system, inducing shivering, sweating, dry throat, paralysis of the tongue and pharynx, followed by irregular breathing, wildly fluctuating heartbeat and, finally, failure of the heart muscles and death. Few victims, including humans, survive.

Most poisonous snake (marine)
Sea snake (Hydrophis belcheri)

Most sea snakes live off the coasts of Asia and northern Australia. Their venom is far more powerful than that of any land snake. Although they are not very aggressive and generally stay in deeper waters, stormy weather and monsoons may bring them closer to the shore where they have been known to bite bathers. They are also occasionally found trapped in fishing nets.

Most poisonous snake (terrestrial)
Taipan (Oxyuranus scutellatus)

The taipan grows to some 11 ft (3.3 m) and inhabits Australia and New Guinea. Its bite causes blood-clotting leading to general paralysis and is fatal within minutes.

Longest fangs
Gaboon viper (Bitis gabonica)
Up to 2 in (5 cm)

The Gaboon viper is a native of tropical north Africa and grows to about 6 ft 3 in (2 m) long, with its body some 6 in (15 cm) in diameter. It is the largest of the vipers and brightly coloured with yellow, purple and brown markings. The viper's extremely long fangs pose a danger not only to other creatures but also to itself, as they may become embedded in its own flesh when the snake misses its strike.

Largest reptile
Komodo dragon (Varanus komodoensis)
Up to 10 ft (3 m) long, 135 lb (61 kg) weight

The komodo dragon is a type of monitor lizard and inhabits a few small islands in Indonesia. It was not discovered and classified until 1912. Despite its size, the komodo can run very fast and is a dangerous predator. It will readily attack large animals such as pigs, deer and buffaloes. Its method is simple: it bites through the tendons on the animal's legs and brings it to the ground. The komodo dragon has a voracious appetite and will devour its own kind as well as eating carrion, when available. It is now an endangered species.

Largest spider
Goliath bird-eating spider (Theraphosa leblondi)
Up to 10 in (25 cm) diameter

The Goliath spider lives in the South American rainforests, particularly around the Amazon basin, and the Guianas. It consumes birds, insects, frogs, toads, mice and lizards. In captivity, the spiders can grow even larger; claims have been made for a 11 in (25.5 cm) legspan and a weight of 6 oz (170 g).

Smallest spider
Patu marplesi
0.1 in (2.5 mm)

This microscopic spider is a native of western Samoa.

Largest spider's web
Orb-weaving spiders
Up to 5 ft (1.5 m) diameter, up to 20 ft (6 m) supporting threads

There are some 2500 species of orb-weaving spider, widely spread throughout the world. The tropical orb-weavers, however, produce the largest webs, made from very strong silk which is a beautiful golden colour. Attempts were made to breed the spiders and use the silk for manufacturing fabric, but they proved difficult to rear and tended to eat each other. Their extraordinary webs have been called 'the crowning glory of arachnid engineering'. Firstly, the spider lays down strong boundary threads, followed by spokes radiating from the centre, where a small platform is constructed. A spiral thread connects the spokes and, when complete, the spider sits on the platform, or hides nearby, holding a signal thread which vibrates when prey falls or blunders into the web. The common British garden spider, whilst not so ambitious as its tropical cousins, is also an orb-weaving spider; fine examples of its work can best be seen in bushes on dewy autumn mornings.

Most poisonous spider
Brazilian huntsman (Phoneutria fera)

The Brazilian huntsman is a member of the Ctenidae family, a small group of mainly tropical and subtropical spiders, known as wandering spiders. They are fairly large in size and usually found in foliage and on the ground. Normally they pose no real threat to humans, but they sometimes hide in clothes and shoes and can inflict several painful poisonous bites when disturbed. If treated promptly with the anti-venom, the bite will not prove fatal.

Largest scorpion

Emperor (imperial) scorpion (Pandinus imperator)

Up to 8 in (20 cm) long

Scorpions are classed, like spiders, as arachnids, and are one of the oldest arthropod groups (which includes insects and crustaceans). Fossil finds indicate that they existed over 300 million years ago in the Silurian period. Scorpions inhabit mainly hot, dry regions such as north Africa, the Middle East, Asia, Australia and the Americas.

Smallest scorpion

Microbothus pusillus

$1/2$ in (13 mm) long

Scorpions have elongated bodies and a segmented tail which ends in a sharp stinger. They have four pairs of legs, variously used for walking and for grasping and tearing apart their prey. Large prey is usually paralyzed by the venom in the stinger before the scorpion tears it apart and sucks out the juices. The female scorpion often eats the male after mating and the young are born alive, attaching themselves to the mother's back for several days thereafter.

Most poisonous scorpion
Fat-tailed scorpion (Androctonus australis)

The fat-tailed scorpion of Tunisia produces a neurotoxin (nerve poison) which causes paralysis of the heart and respiratory muscles and can prove fatal to children and old people. Many scorpions can inflict painful stings, but most are not dangerous. Those that are include *Tityus* in Brazil, *Centruroides* in Mexico and the USA and *Androctonus* in north Africa. Most scorpions prefer flight to fight and will only sting humans if provoked.

Longest insect
Stick insects (Palophus, Pharnacia)
Up to 1 ft 1 in (33 cm) long

Leaf-eating stick insects are superbly adapted to their environment; their body shape and colour reflects that of the twigs and branches they live amongst, and they carry warts and spines on their skin resembling buds and prickles. Most stick insects (also called walkingsticks) are nocturnal feeders and remain absolutely motionless during the day. Their eggs are tiny, seedlike and hard-shelled and many of the 2000 species reproduce by parthenogenesis (the female or, very rarely, the male, lays fertile eggs without mating). Stick insects are found mainly in tropical regions, the USA, Australia, New Zealand and southern Europe.

Smallest insect
Feather-winged beetles (Nanosella fungi)
0.01 in (0.25 mm) long

These minute insects belong to the Coleoptera order, the largest order in the animal kingdom (there are some 330,000 known species). They are known as feather-winged beetles because the membrane on the wings has been replaced with a dense layer of fringed hairs. Feather-wings live in tropical regions and are the smallest of the 350 insect species of the Ptiliidae family, some of which can grow up to 0.08 in (2 mm) long. Feather-winged beetles inhabit rotting wood, fungi, manure, ant nests or the bark of trees, and are sometimes known as fungus beetles.

Heaviest insect
African goliath beetle (Goliathus giganteus)
Up to 4 in (10 cm) long, up to 3^1/$_2$ oz (99 g) weight

The goliath beetle has black leathery wings, bigger

than those of a small bird. It lives in equatorial
Africa.

Insect with shortest life span
Mayfly (Cloeon dipterum)
Lifespan of a few hours as mature adult

Mayflies live underwater as grubs or nymphs,
feeding on water plants. They are a popular food
source for fish – a fact which anglers have taken
advantage of by using fishing flies that resemble
them. After two to three years, the nymph comes
to the surface of the water, its skin splits and it
emerges in its adult form as a mayfly. The insect
sheds its skin once more and then flies away. The
mayfly has two pairs of transparent wings (it is
related to the dragonfly) and is very fragile. It
cannot feed in its adult form – there are only traces
of mouth parts – and it lives long enough only to
mate and lay eggs. There are around 2000 known
species of mayfly and they are found all over the
world.

Most destructive insect ever known
Desert locust (Schistocera gregaria)

Locusts are a type of desert grasshopper and
inhabit Africa, the Middle East and parts of Asia.
They gather in huge swarms, numbering up to 1000

million individuals, each about 2 in (5 cm) long. Such a swarm needs to consume over 3 tons (3.048 tonnes) of food a day to survive. They devastate huge areas of crops and wild vegetation, destroying everything in their path before moving on. Locusts are the most serious pests humans have ever had to contend with and records of their destruction date back thousands of years; perhaps the most famous infestation was that of the plague of locusts mentioned in the Old Testament of the Bible.

Precious Stones
and Gold

Largest diamond
Cullinan
3,106 carats* 1¹/₄ lb (621 g)

The Cullinan diamond was mined on 26 January 1905 in Pretoria, South Africa. Named after Thomas Cullinan, a prospector, it was bought by the Transvaal government and presented to King Edward VII as a token of loyalty to the British crown. It was cut into nine principal stones, of which Cullinan I, the 'Great Star of Africa' (74 facets), was set into the British royal sceptre, and Cullinan II (64 facets) into the Imperial State Crown. Both of these can be seen in the Tower of London. Diamonds are the hardest of all gems (10 on Mohs' scale) and were formed from carbon millions of years ago. The word 'diamond' comes from the Greek *adamastos* meaning 'inflexible, immovable'. Attributed with magical and healing powers from ancient times, diamonds are said to bring energy, strength, beauty and long life to their wearers.

Most famous diamond in the world
Koh-i-Noor
108.93 carats* ³/₄ oz (21.8 g)

This magnificent stone (its name means 'mountain of light') has been the subject of many stories, legends and myths over the centuries. Its first known appearance was in the 14th century, among the jewels of the Rajah of Mawa, then it fell into the hands of the great Prince Babur, founder of the Mogul Empire and known as the 'Lion of the North'. When the last Mogul was finally defeated in battle, he hid the diamond in his turban, only to be betrayed by a trusted aide, who told his conqueror, Nader Shah. When Nader Shah offered to meet the Mogul and exchange turbans with him to seal the peace between them, the Mogul had no choice but to do so. Eventually, the stone came into the hands of Ranjit Singh, the 'Lion of the Punjab', who proudly wore it. He died in 1839 and in 1849 Britain took possession of the Punjab, including the king's treasure which was 'formally presented' to Queen Victoria by Dhulip Singh. The diamond was displayed at the Great Exhibition of 1851 and later recut. In 1937 it was set in the Maltese Cross on the crown made for Queen Elizabeth, the Queen Mother, and can be seen in the Tower of London with the crown jewels.

It was said that the owner of the Koh-i-Noor would rule the world, and many legends and myths tell of curses and misfortunes which would befall those who came by it unlawfully. The manner in which it came into the hands of the British caused

In precious stones, a carat defines weight: one carat = 0.2 g or 200 mg

considerable unease at the time, and there have been several attempts to claim rightful ownership over the years. The government of India asked for its return in 1947 and again in 1953, and in 1976 the Prime Minister of Pakistan, Zulfikar Ali Bhutto, made a formal request that it should be returned to his country. Iran also claims rightful ownership, but for the moment at least the Koh-i-Noor remains in British hands.

Largest ruby
Approx 250 carats* 1³/₄ oz (50 g)

The largest known gem-quality ruby is found in the St Wenceslas crown which Charles IV of Luxembourg, King of Bavaria, placed on the skull of the saint in his shrine. Rubies are made of corundum and vary from deep to pale rose-red (the name comes from the Latin *ruber*, meaning 'red'). The most valuable colour is known as 'pigeon-blood' and has a touch of blue. The Indians valued the ruby for its 'inextinguishable fire' and, throughout the ages, it has been credited with special powers, giving its wearers courage and keeping them from harm. Large high-quality rubies are extremely rare (the last one found, the Peace Ruby of 1918, was approximately 41 carats, 0.287 oz/8.2 g), and several famous 'rubies' are not in fact rubies at all, but red spinels. The Black Prince's Ruby and the Timor Ruby, both in the British crown jewels, are examples of red spinels.

Largest emerald (crystal)
16,300 carats* 7.13 lb (3260 g)

This crystal, together with one of 6550 carats, 2.87 lb/1310 g, can be found in the handle of a dagger in the Topkapi Museum in Istanbul, Turkey, famous for its collection of emeralds. Emeralds are made of green beryl, and the name is derived from the Greek *smaragdos*, 'shiny, green stone'. Large perfect stones are extremely rare and are easily fractured when cutting. Their beautiful green colour has long symbolized new growth, hope and renewal, and the stones were much used in church ornaments and jewellery; indeed the Holy Grail itself was supposed to have been carved from a single emerald. A fine example of a cut emerald (1384 carats, 9.69 oz/276.8 g) is the Devonshire emerald from Colombia, which can be seen in the British Museum in London.

Largest sapphire (crystal)
63,000 carats* 27.6 lb (12,600 g)

This magnificent crystal was discovered in Myanmar (formerly Burma) in 1966 and belongs to the state-

*In precious stones, a carat defines weight: one carat = 0.2 g or 200 mg

owned Myanmar Gems Corporation. As with emeralds, large high-quality stones are extremely rare and are equal in value to diamonds of a similar size and quality. Sapphires are made of corundum and the name is derived from the Greek *sappheiros*, 'blue'. The most prized sapphires are blue, but colours can range from white and yellow to violet, green and black. Sapphires are said to heal eye diseases, to give their owners peace and wisdom, and to act as a talisman for travellers, keeping them from harm.

Largest opal
Panther Opal
281,500 carats* 123.1 lb (56.3 kg)

The Panther Opal was mined in Australia at the beginning of the century, during the 'opal rush' in Queensland and New South Wales. This huge block was divided into three pieces of 180,000, 56,500 and 45,000 carats (79 lb, 24.1 lb and 20 lb/36 kg, 11.3 kg and 9 kg). Opals are made from hydrous silica and are unique among gems, being neither completely opaque nor completely transparent. The name is derived from Sanskrit and means 'precious stone'. Colours vary from greenish red (fire opal), black, white (cacholong) to a combination of several colours (harlequin). In the past, opals were said to react to their wearer's emotions by changing colour and to bring beauty, good fortune and happiness. Their modern reputation as bringers of bad luck (the marriages of those who wore opal engagement rings were said to be doomed to failure, for example), may have come from 19th–century France, where stone-cutters and lapidaries complained that the stones broke and fractured easily thus costing them money.

Largest pearl
Hope Pearl
450 carats* 3.15 oz (90 g)

The Hope Pearl is about 2 in (5 cm) long and is named after the banker Henry Philip Hope. Even larger pearls, such as the Pearl of Asia (575 carats, 4.03 oz/115 g) and the Pearl of Allah (32,000 carats, 14 lb/6.4 kg) are cited in some sources. The Persian Gulf is today the world's major pearl-producing area. Pearls are formed within the shells of certain molluscs (such as oysters and mussels) when layers of calcium carbonate form round a foreign body which irritates the animal. Colours can vary from silvery-white and cream to rose, grey and black. The name is derived from the latin for 'pear' and pearls were known as the Daughters of the Sea. Pearls

*In precious stones, a carat defines weight: one carat = 0.2 g or 200 mg

have been greatly prized from ancient times and have frequently featured in religious beliefs. Vishnu, the Hindu god and guardian of the world, gave pearls to his daughter on her wedding day, and the Greeks dedicated pearls to Aphrodite, goddess of love. To the Romans, pearls represented the tears of Venus, goddess of love, and to early Christians, the tears of Adam and Eve. Representing faith, purity and religious devotion, pearls were given to young girls on their first communion. Medicinally, they were believed to be a remedy for madness.

Largest mass of gold
Holtermann Nugget
4 ft 9 in (145 cm) high, 1 ft 3 in (38 cm) wide, 557³/₄ lb (235 kg) weight

The Holtermann Nugget, a huge lump of mixed slate and gold, was found in Hill End, New South Wales, Australia in 1872. It yielded over 197 lb (90 kg) of pure gold.

Largest nugget
Welcome Stranger
150.9 lb (69 kg)

The largest gold nugget ever found came to light quite by accident, exposed in the ruts of a cart track near Dunolly, Victoria, Australia in 1869. Gold is a heavy, soft metal (between $2^1/_2$ and 3 on Mohs' hardness scale) and is one of only two metals that, in its pure form, is neither grey nor white (copper is the other). The purity of gold is expressed in carats on a scale of 24, where 24 is pure gold. Gold is often mixed with other metals to make it easier to work with, especially for jewellery. Gold has always been highly valued and several monetary systems used the 'gold standard' as their base. This means that the standard unit of currency is a specific weight of gold – originally gold coins were used, but today paper money represents a fixed weight of gold.

Countries of the
World

Largest country
Russian Federation
6,592,800 miles^2 (17.075,352 km^2)

The population of the Russian Federation is approximately 149,000,000 and includes 75 different races. Russians make up the majority with Tartars the second largest group. Most of the people live west of the Ural mountains where the weather is not as severe as in more northern areas. As a result of the 1917 Russian revolution, Russia became part of the Union of Soviet Socialist Republics (USSR) from 1922 to the dissolution of the USSR in 1991. The capital is Moscow.

Smallest country
Vatican City State
0.2 miles^2 (0.51 km^2)

Vatican City State is an independent country within the city of Rome. It lies on the west bank of the River Tiber and is bounded by medieval and Renaissance walls on three sides. Founded in 1929, Vatican City State has its own coinage, postal, telephone and banking systems. It has no income tax, no restrictions on movement of money, and banking operations are strictly secret. Vatican City is the residence of the pope, head of the Roman Catholic Church. The pope has absolute power over the administration of this tiny country and appoints all the government officers. The population is about 1000.

Country with highest population
China (excluding Taiwan)
1,208,842,000

The People's Republic of China has an area of approximately 3,705,408 miles^2 (9,597,006 km^2). Western China is an almost empty land of deserts, mountains and barren plateaus, so most people live in eastern China. Chinese civilization is one of the most ancient in the world and the Chinese invented many things we still use today, such as paper, porcelain and the compass. The Chinese government has introduced policies to try and curb the population growth, penalizing couples who have more than one child.

Country with lowest population
Vatican City State
Approx 1000

See opposite, Smallest country.

Most densely populated country
Monaco
31,000 people per 0.4 miles^2 (20,800 people per km^2)

Monaco-Ville is the capital of this small principality on the Mediterranean coast, whose land joins French territory on every side. The economy depends on property, finance and tourism and favourable tax laws encourage wealthy foreigners to make their homes there.

Most sparsely populated country
Greenland
1 person per 15.1 miles^2 (1 person per 39.1 km^2)

The population of Greenland is just under 56,000 and the area is 840,000 miles^2 (2,175,600 km^2). It is an internally self-governing part of Denmark; Greenland has its own government and sends two members to the Danish parliament. Most people live in the coastal regions – only 16 per cent of the country is ice-free – and the economy depends on the traditional industries of fishing, sealing and reindeer breeding, plus the exploitation of the country's mineral resources such as lead, zinc, iron ore, oil and gas. The capital is Nuuk (Godthåb) and the population is made up of indigenous Eskimos (Inuit) and Danish settlers.

Highest life expectancy (female)
85.3 years
Republic of San Marino (UK 80 years)

The population of San Marino, the third smallest independent country in Europe after Vatican City State and Monaco, is about 25,000 and the area about 23 miles^2 (61 km^2). San Marino retained its independence after Italian unification in 1871 and is surrounded by Italian territory. The country originally developed from a settlement near the Monastery of St Marinus on the slopes of Monte Titano.

Highest life expectancy (male)
77.1 years
Iceland (UK 75 years)

Iceland is a large island in the northern Atlantic Ocean. It lies just outside the Arctic circle and is made up of the coastal lowlands and a central barren plateau, one eighth of which is covered with glaciers. The plateau is mountainous with active volcanoes, geysers and hot springs. Over 50 per cent of the population lives in and around the capital, Reykjavik. Iceland is a very prosperous country with a high standard of living and excellent health and education services. Agriculture and sea fishing are the main industries and although oil must be imported, the Icelanders can use the plentiful supplies of geothermal energy for heating and power.

Lowest life expectancy (male and female)

Rwanda

36.4 years female, 35.9 years male (UK 80 years female, 75 years male)

Rwanda is a small republic in central Africa. Most people are poor peasant farmers, and the country's infrastructure (roads, railways, communications) is very undeveloped. When the country became independent in 1962 (it was formerly administered by Belgium), civil war flared up between the Tutsi (Watutsi) and Hutu people and continued to do so from time to time, damaging the country's already fragile economy. In 1994, the Rwandan president was assassinated and the civil war was resumed; mass killings, mainly of Tutsis by Hutus, followed and huge numbers of refugees made their escape into neighbouring countries, such as Tanzania and Zaire. The situation continues to be unstable, and there seems little prospect, at the moment, of improving the health and welfare conditions of the Rwandan people.

Country with youngest population (percentage of population under 15)

Marshall Islands

51 per cent

The Marshall Islands form an independent republic in the central Pacific. The islands are two parallel chains of coral atolls, more than 1200 in number, the best-known of which is probably Bikini Atoll, used for nuclear testing by the United States in the 1950s. The indigenous people are Micronesians and the population is around 58,000. The Marshall Islanders have large families (the average number of births for a woman of childbearing age is seven) and the doubling time for the population is only 18 years.

Country with oldest population (percentage of people over 75)
Monaco
10.8 per cent

See Most densely populated country, p.121.

Richest country
Luxembourg
£24,900 GNP per head (US$39,850)

The GNP (Gross National Product) is a very rough measure of the annual average national income per person. Luxembourg is a small landlocked country of some 999 miles^2 (2587 km^2), lying between Belgium, France and Germany. The only large town is also called Luxembourg. The economy depends on farming and manufacturing, and the infrastructure (roads, railways, communications) is well-organized. Luxembourg is an independent Grand Duchy with a population of around 381,000.

Poorest country
Rwanda and Mozambique
£50 GNP per head (US$80)

The GNP (Gross National Product) is a very rough measure of the annual average national income per person. For Rwanda, see Lowest life expectancy (male and female), p.124. Mozambique, on the coast of southeast Africa, is a former Portuguese colony which became independent in 1975. Most of the people live on the coastal plain or in the river valleys – including the Limpopo and the Zambesi. The northern highlands have dense, tropical rainforests and rich and varied wildlife, including lions, leopards, hippopotamus, buffalo, giraffe and crocodiles. The country's main products are shrimps, cashew nuts, cotton, sugar and timber. Unfortunately, years of civil war since independence have taken their toll on the economy, which was further shaken by a severe drought and subsequent famine in 1992.

Largest city
Mexico City, Mexico
Population 15,000,000

Mexico City is built on the site of the ancient Aztec capital, Tenochtitlan. It lies at an altitude of 7350 ft (2240 m) and there has been a city here for many hundreds of years. Mexico City is the country's industrial, banking and financial centre.

Largest city in Europe
Paris, France
Population 9,300,000

Paris, on the river Seine, has a history which goes back over 2000 years. The island in the middle of the Seine, Île de la Cité, was a crossing point over the river and was fortified by the Parisii, a Gallic tribe who connected the island to the banks of the river with wooden bridges. In the 19th century, Napoleon III and his architect, Georges Haussmann, replaced the crowded, narrow and unhygienic streets with wide, airy boulevards and avenues. Twentieth-century developments have brought skyscrapers and blocks of flats, as in every major city, although the 1980s and 1990s have included massive, innovative building projects like the Pompidou Centre for the Arts, national library and opera house. The population of Paris is made up of some two million residents of the centre, Ville de Paris, and the seven million residents of the 20 districts (*arrondissements*).

Largest city in the UK
London, England
Population 7,000,000

London (Londinium) on the River Thames was founded by the Romans in about AD 43. William the Conqueror made it the capital of England and was crowned in Westminster Abbey in 1066. In the 19th century, London was the world's largest city and centre of the British Empire. London is composed of the City of London (now mainly offices) and 32 boroughs, which make up Greater London.

Largest city in North America
Mexico City, Mexico
Population 15,000,000

See Largest city, p.126.

Largest city in South America
Buenos Aires, Argentina
Population 10,000,000

Buenos Aires ('Fair Winds') was first settled by Europeans in 1580 and lies 124 miles (199.6 km) from the sea on the Rio de la Plata (River Plate). Its harbour is entirely man-made and is Argentina's chief port. Buenos Aires is the business and financial centre of the country and is noted for its beautiful buildings and well-kept parks and gardens.

Largest city in Africa
Cairo, Egypt
Population 13,000,000

Cairo, on the River Nile, was the centre of the Ancient Egyptian civilization, and modern Cairo dates back to the 10th century. After Saladin defeated the crusaders in the 12th century, he made Egypt the most powerful Muslim state in the world and over the next two centuries Cairo grew to be the largest city in both Europe and Africa. The Ottoman rulers of the 19th century modernized old Cairo and went on to create an entirely new city near the old one, largely following European architectural styles; this has become the present-day centre of Cairo. The city has grown rapidly in the 20th century and remains the most important centre for trade between Europe, the Middle East and North Africa.

Largest city in Asia
Bombay, India
Population 12,500,000

Bombay is the financial, trading and film industry centre of India. It was originally built on seven small islands, joined by bridges and causeways, which link them all. One quarter of the city lies below sea level, on a low-lying, reclaimed plain called Bombay Island. Bombay has an excellent harbour and grew rapidly after the opening of the Suez Canal in 1869. It is known as the 'Gateway to India' and is one of the most densely populated cities in the world.

Largest city in Australasia
Sydney, Australia
Population 3,770,000

Sydney is famed for its magnificent harbour, which has one of the world's largest dry docks, the beautiful steel arch Sydney Harbour Bridge and the opera house. Sydney is highly industrialized with almost one quarter of Australia's factories within its boundaries. The city was founded in 1788 by a group of convicts and soldiers who came ashore nearby. It was the first European settlement in Australia and was named after Viscount Sydney, the British government minister responsible for colonial affairs at the time.

Human Life and
Society

Tallest known person
Robert Pershing Wadlow
8 ft 11 in (2.71 m)

Wadlow was born in Illinois, USA, and died in 1940 at the age of 22. Acromegaly or gigantism is a rare abnormality of growth which causes the sufferer to grow to an excessive height. The underlying medical cause is a pituitary tumour which secretes an excess of growth hormone. People with acromegaly are not physically strong and may have a shortened life expectancy.

Shortest known person
Gul Mohammed
22¹/₂ in (56.3 cm)

Mohammed was born in India in 1957 and died in 1997. Like gigantism, dwarfism or restricted growth can be caused by hormonal disturbances or problems with the pituitary gland, but it can also be inherited.

Longest bone in the body
Femur

The femur is a legbone, which joins the hip joint to the knee joint. The 206 bones of the human body support and protect the vital organs. A healthy human bone is almost as strong as cast iron or steel, but only a fraction of their weight. Bones are made out of collagen (a protein) and minerals containing calcium and phosphorus. The centre of many bones consists of bone marrow, through which run the blood vessels that supply the bones with food and oxygen. Red and white blood cells are also made in the bone marrow. Bones are connected to each other by joints, enabling movement: hinge-type joints are found in the fingers, for example, whereas ball-and-socket joints, which enable greater movement, are found at the shoulder and the hip. Bones can repair and regenerate themselves when damaged.

Largest organ in the human body
Skin
$21^1/_2$ ft^2 (2 m^2) per average adult

All vertebrates (animals with backbones) have skin, although the outer covering is different in different species (scales, hair, feathers, etc.). The skin is a multifunctional organ, protecting body tissues against injury, regulating body temperature and providing a waterproof outer layer. Nerves in the skin, 'touch receptors', are constantly sending messages to the brain – there are some 200 of these per 0.15 in^2 (1 cm^2). The skin is composed of three layers, the epidermis, dermis and subcutaneous fatty tissue. The epidermis is constantly flaking off and being replaced and the entire surface is renewed in this way once every six weeks.

Largest constituent of the human body
Water
60.8 pints (38 litres) per average adult

Water is the main component of blood and the average adult has between 6.2–10.6 pints (3.5–6 litres) of blood. Each day the body loses about 0.44 pints (0.25 litres) in sweat.

Oldest known person
Jeanne Louise Calment
122 years (died 1997)

Oldest known person in UK
Lucy Askew
114 years (died 1997)

Most children in a single birth (surviving)
Seven (4 boys, 3 girls)

The McCaughey septuplets were born on 19 November 1997 in Des Moines, Iowa, USA. The babies were carried for longer than 31 weeks (the longest-known period for such a large multiple pregnancy), and all seven babies weighed more than the critical weight of 2 lb (0.9 kg). The babies were born by Caesarian section and immediately placed in incubators. Only five days later one of the boys was able to breathe on his own.

Oldest known mother
A son, born in July 1994. The mother is said to have undergone fertility treatment.

Oldest known mother in the UK
Elizabeth Buttle, England, 60
A son, born in January 1998. The mother is said to have undergone fertility treatment.

Most common cause of death (developed countries)
Diseases of the circulatory system (heart disease and stroke)
These so-called 'diseases of civilization', such as coronary heart disease, are associated with over-

eating, lack of exercise and smoking. The commonest type of heart disease causes narrowing and stiffening of the coronary arteries (those that supply the heart muscle with blood). If an artery is completely blocked by a blood clot, then the heart muscle is damaged and the heart itself may fail. A reduction of blood flow to a part of the brain, resulting from the lodging of a blood clot in an artery in the brain, is described as a stroke; temporary or permanent paralysis of parts of the body may result.

Most common cause of sudden death (developed countries)
Coronary heart disease (ischaemic heart disease)

See Most common cause of death (developed countries), p.135.

Country with highest death rate from circulatory diseases
Hungary
676 per 100,000 (UK 507 per 100,000) population

Country with lowest death rate from circulatory diseases

Japan
144 per 100,000 (UK 507 per 100,000)
population

Rarest disease

Smallpox (variola)

Smallpox was officially declared eradicated in 1980. Throughout history, smallpox has killed vast numbers of people (60 million in the 18th century alone). The World Health Organization pledged to eradicate smallpox, particularly in the developing world, through a world vaccination programme using jet injector guns with high-pressure sprays instead of needles, thus allowing large numbers to be vaccinated very quickly. Immunization against smallpox is long lasting because there is no animal 'reservoir' for the virus. Smallpox causes fever, muscle pains and a severe rash of weeping pustules which leave deep, pitted scars; it is often, but not always, fatal. Some smallpox cultures are still kept in laboratories for research purposes. See also First vaccine, p.139.

Most common disease
Common cold
There are almost 200 different rhinoviruses which cause the common cold and, as they have a tendency to mutate, their numbers are constantly increasing. Colds are found everywhere in the world except Antarctica and are transmitted by direct contact or through the air by sneezing and coughing.

Most recently discovered disease
New strain of Creutzfeldt-Jacob Disease (CJD)
Creutzfeldt-Jacob Disease causes dementia (mental deterioration) and is irreversible and always fatal. The new strain may possibly be transmitted to humans by eating meat infected with BSE (bovine spongiform encephalitis), a similar disease which affects cows.

Most rapidly-increasing disease
Tuberculosis
Tuberculosis kills more people every year than AIDS and malaria combined. Once the scourge of western industrialized societies, particularly in the 19th century, the disease is spreading rapidly in

developing countries and has also begun to reappear in the west, especially in impoverished inner-city areas. Humans are usually infected by the *mycobacterium tuberculosis* bacillus, which is air-borne and expelled from the lungs of infected people, but can also be infected by the bovine variety, *mycobacterium bovis*, taken in by drinking the milk of infected cows. The air-borne bacilli affect the lungs, causing lumps or tubercles to form; the lungs become scarred, the patient's health deteriorates and there is a persistent cough. Whole areas of the lungs are slowly destroyed, the patient suffers considerable pain and coughs up blood, becoming weaker and weaker before dying from general debility. The bovine form of the disease affects the bones and joints; only about 10 per cent of human tuberculosis is caused by this form. TB can be detected by X-ray and skin tests and can be treated effectively with drugs and general care. A vaccine is available. Louis Pasteur (1822–95), the French scientist, invented a method of heat-treating milk, now known as past-eurization, which kills the bovine bacillus.

First vaccine
Smallpox (variola) 1796

Sometime in 1796 the English physician, Edward Jenner (1749–1823), heard rumours that farm workers who came into close contact with cattle suffering from cowpox seemed to be unaffected by the disease themselves. At the time smallpox was a terrible scourge in western Europe: in Britain alone, 30 per cent of children died from it before they reached the age of three, and many more were left badly scarred, weak and blind. Acting on these rumours, Jenner introduced some pus taken from a cow infected with cowpox into the skin of a small boy and monitored his progress. The boy stayed healthy. Jenner concluded that the cowpox virus had been weakened by being passed first through the cow's immune system. When this weakened virus was introduced into the human body, its immune system was able effectively to attack the weakened viral cells. The antibodies produced to attack the weakened cowpox virus were then able to destroy the stronger smallpox virus.

First recognized surgical operation using anaesthetic

Removal of a tumour using ether, October 1846, Boston, USA

This surgical procedure was performed by William Thomas Morton on Gilbert Abbott and took place at Massachusetts General Hospital before an audience. The idea of using anaesthetics to relieve pain during operations had already been explored for centuries. Various substances had been considered, including opium, henbane, mandrake and alcohol. In 1799 the British scientist, Sir Humphry Davy (inventor of the miners' safety lamp), noticed that inhaling nitrous oxide ('laughing gas'), made him feel lighthearted and happy (as well as relieving his toothache). As word spread of this new phenomenon, laughing gas parties became the fashion, even spreading across the the Atlantic to America. Then ether (made by the reaction of sulphuric acid with ethanol) was found to have similar properties and ether parties supplanted laughing gas parties as the new diversion for the wealthy and fashionable. Showmen offered 'ether frolics' as public entertainment: volunteers were given small doses of ether and when they fell over, through taking in too much of the drug, they were shown to have felt no pain. At the same time, of course, more serious medical and scientific experiments were taking place, using both animal and human subjects. Horace Wells, from Hartford, Connecticut, USA, staged public demonstrations using nitrous oxide to anaesthetize patients who were having teeth extracted. Medical opinion was very sceptical and when, on one occasion, Wells did not give his patient sufficient nitrous oxide, his claims that he could perform painless operations were ridiculed and mocked by the medical profession. Wells, disillusioned and bitter, became a chloroform* salesman. He soon became addicted to the drug and died in jail after throwing sulphuric acid at two women. William Morton, a former partner of Wells, had studied medicine and was a qualified dentist. He took up Wells' work where he had left off and continued to research and develop the use of anaesthetics in surgical procedures, preferring ether to nitrous oxide because of its longer-lasting power.

First antibiotic
Penicillin, 1928

Alexander Fleming (1881–1955), the Scots bacteriologist, was working in the Inoculation Department of St Mary's Hospital, London, when he discovered, almost by chance, the power of penicillin to kill bacteria without harming the body. A culture dish containing live staphylococci bacteria (which cause blood poisoning and boils), had been contaminated by airborne mould spores, perhaps from other experiments in an adjacent laboratory. Fleming noticed that the mould growing in the dish

*The possibilities of using chloroform (trichloromethane) as an anaesthetic were also being explored at this time, but its limited effects (10–15 min), and extremely narrow safety margin for dosage, precluded its use in most operations; it was, however, an effective pain reliever in childbirth.

had killed the staphylococci bacteria where it had come into contact with them. The mould was called *Penicillium notatum*. Fleming tried various experiments with the mould, but did not use it on infected animals. Howard Foley (an Australian pathologist) and Ernest Chain (biochemist) developed Fleming's research and, with the biochemist Norman Wheatley, discovered how to mass produce and store penicillin as a usable drug. In 1941, the first human patients were treated and in 1945 Fleming, Florey and Chain shared the Nobel prize for medicine.

First successful organ transplant
Kidney, 1954, Boston, Massachusetts, USA

A 24-year-old man received a kidney from his twin brother.

First heart transplant
3 December 1967, Groote Schuur Hospital, Cape Town, South Africa

The heart of a 24-year-old woman, who had died from head injuries in a car accident, was transplanted by surgeon Christiaan Barnard (born 1922) into Louis Washkansky (54), who had had three major heart attacks since 1959 and was dying of heart failure. Washkansky died 18 days later from a lung infection. The post mortem revealed that the heart had functioned well until the end.

Longest-reigning monarch in European history

Louis XIV of France, 1643–1715 (72 years)

Louis XIV (1638-1715) came to power at the age of four years and eight months. His early years were dominated by Cardinal Mazarin, who wielded absolute power and control over Louis. When Mazarin died in 1661, the king (aged 23), informed his ministers that he would now assume absolute control over his kingdom. Louis believed in the divine (God-given) right of kings to do exactly what they wanted; he believed he was God's representative on earth and was responsible only to God for his actions. As far as his people were concerned, they had no democratic rights at all, and if they were disobedient to their king, they were disobedient to God himself. Louis was not much interested in the welfare of his people; he effectively disabled Parliament and his court was isolated and far removed from their everyday concerns. Recognizing that the nobles could form an effective opposition against his power, Louis created a splendid and extravagant court at which they were invited to spend their time – gambling, eating, drinking and indulging in all kinds of dissipation. Thus the influence of the nobles was weakened and Louis' power was supreme. A great patron of the arts, Louis built the vast court at Versailles and encouraged writers such as Racine and Molière. Although he was accused of ruining the country through his extravagance and his constant wars with neighbouring countries in an attempt to consolidate French supremacy, Louis, the Sun King, left an invaluable artistic legacy to the French people.

Longest-reigning monarch in the UK
Victoria, 1837–1901 (64 years)

Queen Victoria (1819–1901) was the daughter of Edward, Duke of Kent, fourth son of George IV, and the German Princess Victoria. She became queen at the age of 18 and immediately became popular. Victoria married the German Prince Albert in 1840; they were very happy together and produced nine children. Victoria was devastated by Albert's death in 1861 at the age of 42 and shut herself away from the public, causing considerable adverse criticism and even the birth of a republican movement. Encouraged by the prime minister, Benjamin Disraeli, the queen slowly emerged from her seclusion and was made Empress of India amid great splendour in 1876. The Golden Jubilee, celebrating 50 years of her rule in 1887, marked the zenith of British power and wealth. Victoria's presence so marked the 19th century that her name has become synonymous with it.

First British prime minister
Robert Walpole

Sir Robert Walpole (1676–1745) is widely accepted as having established the office and role of prime minister, although this title did not exist at the time. The son of a Norfolk gentleman, Walpole became a member of parliament when he was 25, rising to prominence when he rescued the national economy from the disastrous results of the 'South Sea Bubble' financial fiasco. His reward was to become Chancellor of the Exchequer and First Lord of the Treasury in 1721. Walpole was supported by both George I and George II, but George II's son Frederick, Prince of Wales, did all he could to undermine Walpole's power and his popularity declined. In 1742 Walpole was defeated and he retired from politics. Although Walpole recognized the growing influence of the House of Commons in formulating government policies, he made extensive personal use of government patronage (offering titles, jobs or gifts to gain someone's support) to ensure he got sufficient backing for his plans. He will always be remembered for saying 'All men have their price'.

Youngest British prime minister
William Pitt the Younger
Prime minister in 1783, aged 24

William Pitt (1759–1806) was instrumental in reorganizing Britain's finances, but he never fulfilled his other aims of reforming parliament and achieving Catholic emancipation (at this time, Roman Catholics were not allowed to hold public office or become members of parliament). The French revolution caused considerable apprehension in Britain, which was soon involved in wars with France, and this encouraged Pitt to support repressive policies against radical opposition. He also introduced income tax at a rate of 10 per cent to pay for the army and navy. Pitt was instrumental in drawing up the Act of Union with Ireland in 1800 and, in his second term of office (1804–06), he organized an alliance with Russia and Austria against Napoleon. See also Youngest graduate in the UK, p.153.

Longest-serving British prime minister
Robert Banks Jenkinson
2nd Earl of Liverpool, Prime Minister 1812–27

The Earl of Liverpool (1770–1828) came to power after the death of Spencer Perceval (see below, First British prime minister to be assassinated). Liverpool steered the country through the war with America in 1812 and the final campaigns of the Napoleonic wars. At the Congress of Vienna in 1814–15, Liverpool supported the abolition of the slave trade, although he was less liberal in his policies at home. The early 19th century was marked by industrial and agricultural change and unrest, to which Liverpool's government responded by introducing repressive measures, such as suspending *habeas corpus* (the right not to be imprisoned without trial) in 1817.

First British prime minister to be assassinated
Spencer Perceval
Murdered on 11 May 1812

Spencer Perceval (1762–1812) was a lawyer and member of parliament for Northampton. He was a strong supporter of William Pitt, rising quickly to high office and becoming Chancellor of the Exchequer in 1807 and prime minister in 1809. Perceval was shot in the House of Commons entrance by a bankrupt banker from Liverpool, John Bellingham, who was later hanged for his crime.

First female prime minister
Sirimavo Bandaranaike
Prime minister of Sri Lanka (1960–65, 1970–77, 1994–)

Sirimavo Bandaranaike (born 1916) was married to the politician S.W.R.D. Bandaranaike in 1940, and when he was assassinated in 1959 she became party leader. Her Sri Lanka Freedom Party won a decisive victory in the General Election of July 1960 and she became the world's first female prime minister. Defeated in the next general election, her party subsequently rose to power as part of a socialist coalition, but a combination of repressive policies and ethnic rivalries, together with increasing problems for the Sri Lankan economy, brought her government to a decisive defeat in the general election of July 1977. Mrs Bandaranaike was later stripped of her rights but these were restored by J.R. Jayawardene, Sri Lankan president, in 1986.

First female prime minister in Europe
Margaret Thatcher
Prime minister of the United Kingdom (1979–90)

Margaret Thatcher (born 1925) is the daughter of a grocer and comes from Grantham, Lincolnshire, England. She studied chemistry and law and was elected to parliament in 1959 as Conservative member for Finchley, London. Thatcher became party leader then prime minister when her party won the general elections of 1979, 1983 and 1987. Thatcher (now Lady Thatcher) held strong views on political principles and policies and exerted considerable control over her ministers. She was known as the 'Iron Lady' and her distinctive approach to government is known as 'Thatcherism'.

First female member of parliament to take her seat (House of Commons)*
Viscountess (Nancy) Astor
Member of parliament for Plymouth, 1919

Nancy Langhorne of Virginia, USA (1879–1964), was first married at the age of 18 but divorced her husband six years later. In 1906 she married Waldorf Astor, a member of the fabulously wealthy American Astor family. His father had become a British citizen in 1899 and subsequently a viscount. Nancy Astor herself became a British citizen and, when her husband inherited his father's title and resigned his seat in the House of Commons to become a member of the House of Lords, she took

*Constance Gore-Booth (Countess Markievicz) (1868–1927) was elected in 1918 to represent St Patrick's Division, Dublin, thus making her the first woman to be elected to the British parliament. In accordance with Sinn Fein policy, she did not take up her seat.

his place and was elected as Unionist member for Plymouth in 1919. As an MP, Astor took a great interest in matters involving children, the family and women's welfare and was highly regarded in many spheres of society. The mother of six children, Nancy Astor was re-elected many times before she finally retired in 1945.

Youngest male member of parliament
William Pitt the Younger
Member of parliament in 1781, aged 22

William Pitt was the second son of the Earl of Chatham. He was educated privately, owing to his poor health, until he entered the University of Cambridge at the age of 14. At 17 he graduated and in 1781 became MP for Appleby. See also Youngest British prime minister, p.147 and Youngest graduate in the UK, p.154.

Youngest female member of parliament
*(Josephine) Bernadette Devlin
(McAliskey)*
Member of parliament in 1969, aged 22 years 359 days

As Bernadette Devlin, McAliskey (born 1947) was the member of parliament for Mid-Ulster from 1969 to 1974 and was the youngest member since

William Pitt the Younger (see p.151). In 1971 she gave birth to an illegitimate child and lost the support of many of her Catholic constituents, although she later married. In 1979 McAliskey was unsuccessful in her efforts to become a member of the European parliament. In 1981 she actively supported the IRA hunger strikers, and she and her husband were later shot and wounded in an attempted assassination.

First country to give women the right to vote
New Zealand 1893

First European country to give women the right to vote
Finland 1906

Last European country to give women the right to vote
Liechtenstein 1984

Since 1984 women over 20 years of age are permitted to vote on national, but not local, issues.

Liechtenstein is a small country, lying between Switzerland and Austria. It has an area of only 62 miles^2 (160.6 km^2) and a population of around 27,000. Liechtenstein is governed as a constitutional monarchy, with a hereditary head of state. It has no natural resources of any great value and much of the land is heavily forested and mountainous. The economy depends on light manufacturing, tourism, banking and financial services and special stamp issues.

Youngest undergraduate in the UK
William Thomson
Entered Glasgow University in 1834, aged 10

Scotsman William Thomson (1824–1907) was the son of a Professor of Mathematics at Glasgow University. At 22 he was a Professor of Mathematics and Natural Philosophy. Thomson subsequently had an outstanding career, combining pure and applied science and exploring such concepts as geomagnetism and hydrodynamics. He invented innumerable electrical instruments and his home in Glasgow was the first to be lit by electric light. Thomson was later knighted and become the first Baron Kelvin. He is buried in Westminster Abbey.

Youngest graduate in the UK
William Pitt the Younger
Graduated from Cambridge University in 1781, aged 17

See Youngest British prime minister, Youngest male member of parliament, pp.147 and 151.

Youngest professor in the UK
Colin Maclaurin
Professor of Mathematics, Marischal College, Aberdeen University, September 1717, aged 19

Scotsman Maclaurin graduated from Glasgow University in 1713, then became Professor of Mathematics at Marischal College, Aberdeen University. In 1725, on Isaac Newton's recommendation, Maclaurin was appointed to the Chair of Mathematics at Edinburgh University. In 1745 he helped to organize the city's defences against the Jacobite army, led by Bonnie Prince Charlie.

Richest man
Sir Muda Hassanal Bolkiah Mu'izzaddin Waddaulah, Ruler of Negara Brunei Darussalam
Estimated fortune £19 billion

Commonly known as the Sultan of Brunei, Sir Muda was born in 1946 and has been ruler of Brunei since 1967. Brunei is a small country in the north-east of the island of Borneo. It has valuable offshire oil and gas deposits and thus a very high standard of living. Brunei is a one-party state and the sultan is also prime minister, minister of finance and minister of home affairs, with wide powers to appoint other government officers. It has been estimated that Brunei's oil and gas reserves will begin to decline substantially within the next 20 years.

Richest businessman
Bill Gates
Estimated fortune £18 billion (US$29 billion)

American Gates, founder of the computer software giant Microsoft, sees his fortune increase by some £20 million (US$36 million) each day.

Richest woman
Queen Elizabeth II
Estimated fortune £250 million

The queen is not obliged to publish details of her financial affairs, so no really accurate figures are available. This projected figure excludes the royal art collection which is now in trust. The queen pays around £1 million per year in income tax.

Science, Technology and Communication

Most common element* in the universe
Hydrogen
Atomic number 1 Chemical symbol H

Hydrogen is the most common element in the universe and the third most common element (after oxygen 46.6 per cent and silicon 27.7 per cent) in the earth's crust. The British scientist, Henry Cavendish, is generally accepted as having finally isolated and identified it in 1766. The name is derived from the Greek and means 'water maker' and it is so called because, as Antoine Lavoisier the French chemist discovered, hydrogen always leaves behind a little water after burning. Hydrogen has no taste or smell and is invisible.

Simplest naturally occurring element*
Hydrogen
Atomic number 1 Chemical symbol H

Hydrogen, a colourless gas, has only $1/15$th of the weight of air and is so light that it was often used for fuelling balloons and airships. Nowadays, however, helium, which is twice the weight of hydrogen, is preferred as it will not burn.

An element is a substance which cannot be split into two or more substances by chemical means.

Most complex naturally occurring element*

Uranium
Atomic number 92 Chemical symbol U

Uranium, a silvery-white metallic element, was isolated in 1789 by the German scientist Martin Klaproth, and named after the recently-discovered plant Uranus. Henri Becquerel, the French physicist, found radioactivity in uranium in 1896, and in 1938 Otto Hahn and Fritz Strassmann discovered the phenomenon of nuclear fission by bombarding uranium with slow neutrons. Intensive research followed this discovery and led to the atomic bomb (first test 16 July 1945, first use in warfare 6 August 1945, Hiroshima, Japan), and the use of nuclear power to generate electricity.

Newest elements*

Transuranic elements
Atomic numbers 93–112

The transuranic elements are those which lie beyond uranium, number 92 in the periodic table of the elements. These elements, with the exception of plutonium, neptunium and americium, minute amounts of which have been found in nature, are artificial, radioactive, highly unstable and have life-spans ranging from billions of years to infinitesimal fractions of a second (e.g. element 112 is claimed to have a lifetime of 240 millionths of a second). All transuranic elements are created artificially, using various nuclear reactions (e.g. changing the atoms of one element into those of another by bombarding it with neutrons; thus the number of protons in the nucleus of the atom is changed and a new atom is formed). Since 1964 several groups of scientists have claimed to have created nine 'new' elements, but these have not yet been officially recognized by the International Union of Pure and Applied Chemistry, which currently recognizes 103 elements only. Some scientists predict that new elements will continue to be discovered, possibly up to atomic number 200.

Element* with highest boiling and melting points
Tungsten
Boiling point 10,652 °F (5900 °C)
Melting point 6098 °F (3370 °C)
Atomic number 74 Chemical symbol W

Tungsten or wolfram is a grey, solid metal. *Tungsten* comes from the Swedish, meaning 'heavy

*An element is a substance which cannot be split into two or more substances by chemical means.

stone'. It is both malleable and hard and, alloyed with steel, is used for making the tips of high-speed cutting tools. The pure metal is used as a filament in electric light bulbs. Tungsten was discovered by the Spanish scientists J.J. and F. d'Elhuyar in 1783.

Element* with lowest boiling and melting points

Helium

Boiling point -452.16 °F (-268.98 °C), melting point -520.52 °F (-271.4 °C) at 29.6 atmospheres pressure

Atomic number 2 Chemical symbol He

Helium is a colourless gas. In its liquid form it is the only liquid which cannot be frozen by reducing temperature alone – pressure must also be applied. It is the second most abundant element in the universe. Helium was discovered to be part of the sun's chemical makeup in 1868 and was named after Helios, the Greek god of the sun. In 1895 the British scientist, W. Ramsay, found helium present on earth and it quickly became useful as a non-flammable replacement for hydrogen in balloons and airships. Today, helium is used mainly in meteorological balloons and metallurgical processes such as arc welding.

Lightest metal
Lithium
Atomic number 3 Chemical symbol Li

Lithium, which takes its name from Greek *lithos,* 'stone', is a silvery solid. It was discovered by the Swedish scientist A. Arfvedson in 1817. Lithium is used in industrial processes as a thickener and gelling agent, and has recently been incorporated into drugs to help sufferers from manic depression.

Heaviest metal
Osmium
Atomic number 76 Chemical symbol Os

Osmium, a hard bluish-white metal, was discovered by the British scientist Smithson Tennant in 1804. Its name comes from Greek *osmé,* 'odour', in recognition of its distinctive smell. Combined with platinum, osmium is used to create a very hard alloy, used in instrument pivots and pen tips. Osmium is highly toxic.

First calculator
Blaise Pascal 1642

Pascal (1623–62), the French philosopher and scientist, invented the calculator when he was just 19 to help his father in his work as a local government officer. A bulky mechanical device, it carried out calculations through a sequence of rotating cogwheels and was limited to simple addition and subtraction.

First electronic special-purpose programmable computer

Colossus
December 1943

An important weapon in World War II (1939–45), Colossus was developed by M. Newman and T.H. Flowers and was specifically designed to decipher the codes generated by German electromechanical devices, and known as the Enigma Codes. The first machines became operational in 1943 and contained 1500 vacuum tubes or valves which operated at high speed. By 1944 faster machines containing 2500 tubes increased efficiency.

First electronic general-purpose programmable computer

ENIAC
February 1946

The Electronic Numerical Integrator and Calculator contained 18,000 vacuum tubes and stood 8 ft 3 in (2.5 m) high and 78 ft 9 in (24 m) long. It could do 5000 additions per second (a modern personal computer can carry out 50 million separate tasks in the same time), and was controlled by a program set up externally. ENIAC was built by J.W. Mauchly, J. Presper Eckart and others at the University of Pennsylvania, USA.

First electronic general-purpose stored program computer
'Baby' 1948

'Baby', a massive (17 ft by 8 ft/5.2 by 2.4 m) construction, weighing 1 ton (1.016 tonnes), was developed by F. Williams and T. Kilburn at Manchester University. The computer was able to do various tasks and contained 600 valves and 100 switches; results of its calculations appeared as glowing dots on a cathode ray tube. Program information was stored in a tube 6 in by 18 in (15 cm by 45 cm) and its memory was 128 bytes (compared with 8 million bytes on a modern personal computer).

First commercially-successful microprocessor
8080 Microprocessor
Intel Corporation, USA, 1974

The development of large-scale integration (LSI) made it possible to pack thousands of transistors and other electronic components on to a single computer chip. Thus the microprocessor was born. The 8080 held about 4800 transistors, whereas today's equivalent contains about 3,200,000 transistors.

First personal computer
Apple II
USA, 1977

The Apple Computer Company was founded by Americans Stephen Wozniak and Steven Jobs in 1976. Their Apple II was instantly successful and was followed in 1984 by the Apple Macintosh, a versatile, easy-to-use desktop computer.

Most powerful microprocessor
Incorporating Intel P7 chip
Intel Corporation, USA, 1997

The most powerful microprocessor has demonstrated that it can handle instructions twice as fast as its predecessors. Such performances raise the level of microprocessors to the entry-level of supercomputers, the highly complex and powerful machines used in science and industry.

First supercomputer to beat a world chess champion

Deep Blue, 11 May 1997

Deep Blue beat Grand Master Gary Kasparov in Philadelphia, USA. Of the six games, the computer won two, three were drawn and Kasparov won one. In 1996, Kasparov beat Deep Blue 4–2, but since then its programmers have improved the computer's powers. Kasparov was stunned at his defeat, even though it was by a computer that can 'look' at an average of 200 million possible positions per second!

Largest supercomputer

US Department of Energy Ultra computer
Sandia National Laboratories, New Mexico, USA

Introduced in 1996, this computer has the capacity to carry out 1 trillion calculations per second (teraflops). It is used to develop simulation technologies to ensure the safety and reliability of the US nuclear deterrence without underground testing, as well as providing the power for medical and pharmaceutical research, weather prediction and aircraft and car design.

Largest supercomputer in the UK
T3E Cray Supercomputer
Bracknell, England

The Cray supercomputer is owned and operated by
the Meteorological Office. At the time of writing,
the Cray is the third biggest supercomputer in the
world and is used for weather forecasting. Weather
observations from all over the world are fed into
the computer which converts them into
mathematical equations and then into forecasts.
The Cray can make 80,000 million calculations per
second.

Largest computer network
Internet

A computer network is a group of computers that
can be linked to each other to exchange
information. The Internet grew from the earlier
ARPANET, an experimental network built by the US
Defense Department's Advanced Research Projects
Agency (ARPA), to allow researchers to combine
resources and collaborate with each other from
wherever they happened to be working. Later, this
system was expanded to include communication
between different networks of different types, far
beyond the confines of ARPANET, and thus the
Internet came into existence. The 1990s saw the

rapid growth of commercial Internet-access providers and the World Wide Web, offering users access to information and contacts across the world. The Web was initially created by Tim Berners-Lee who, while working in the European Centre for Nuclear Research (CERN), Geneva, thought it useful for scientists working in different parts of the world to collaborate and share information. As with the Internet, the Web quickly outgrew its initial purpose and soon reached the general public through the ownership of personal computers. There are now thought to be tens of millions of Internet users worldwide and figures are expected to double every year.

First fax transmission
Great Exhibition, London 1851 (successful demonstration)

The idea of a facsimile transmission (ie sending an exact copy of an image or document) originated with Alexander Bain, a Scots inventor, who patented his system in 1842. Bain's apparatus was based on a stylus mounted on a pendulum, and his ideas were taken up and developed by the English physicist, Frederick Blakewell, whose system of receiving and transmitting images on cylinders was used until the 1960s. In 1863 Arthur Korn, a German scientist, began to use a photoelectric cell for transmitting photographs, and by 1906 his equipment was used commercially for transmitting newspaper photographs between Munich and Berlin. The expansion of telephone services in the 20th century opened up new possibilities for faxing, which developed independently in Europe and America. In 1974 the International Telegraph and Telephone Consultative Committee set the first worldwide standard, ensuring compatability between American and European machines. Nowadays, faxes use digital signals and special codes and are extremely fast and accurate. Countless millions of fax machines are now in use worldwide. However, the increasing use of personal computers with modems, which can perform fax tasks, may well make them obsolete in the not-too-distant future.

First transmission of speech by telephone
10 March 1876

'Mr Watson, come here. I want you,' said Scots-born American inventor Alexander Graham Bell (1847–1922), to his assistant, Thomas Watson, waiting in a nearby room. Unremarkable, perhaps, but this first successful transmission of speech by telephone represents a breakthrough in technology without which the telecommunications explosion of the 20th century might never have happened. Bell's family were recognized as leading practitioners in the field of elocution and speech therapy, and Bell himself was particularly interested in developing ways of teaching deaf people to speak. In 1874–75 he began to think about ways of transmitting speech by artificial means and he started working out specifications for what would become the telephone. On 7 March 1876 he was granted US Patent No 174465, often described as the most valuable patent ever. Other people quickly entered into the race to produce the machine commercially, and when Bell Telephone Company began commercial operations the following year, hundreds of lawsuits were immediately filed, both against the company and on its behalf. The next few years were occupied with the most complex and involved patent litigation in history.

First transatlantic radio signal

1901

Poldhu, Cornwall, England, to St John's, Newfoundland, Canada

Guglielmo Marconi (1874–1937) was born in Bologna, Italy, the son of an Italian landowner and an Irish mother. He studied in Florence and Livorno and in 1895 he began to carry out his first experiments in radio transmission. Lack of government support in Italy led him to transfer his work to England. After his successful first transatlantic transmission, Marconi began his own company and established a regular news service between England and America for *The Times* newspaper. A restless and driven man, Marconi continued to search out new possibilities and he did a great deal of work in shortwave and microwave communication systems, as well as on escalators and lifts. He was awarded the Nobel Prize for Physics in 1909.

First gramophone recording
December 1877

'Mary had a little lamb' were the first words to be successfully recorded and played back by Thomas Edison's gramophone. An American scientist and inventor, Thomas Alva Edison (1847–1931) created the first device that could successfully accomplish both recording and playing back. At the time the machines were known as phonographs, used roller-shaped records made of wax and a large funnel-shaped horn. Edison, a man of immense imagination and dedication, went on to patent nearly 1100 inventions, including a light bulb and a dictating machine, the Ediphone. He is famously quoted as saying that genius is '1 per cent inspiration and 99 per cent perspiration'.

First regular television broadcasting service

1936
British Broadcasting Corporation (BBC), London

Scottish inventor John Logie Baird (1888–1946) had demonstrated the first successful television picture (an image of a ventriloquist's dummy) in 1925. His equipment then is said to have included odd bits and pieces such as old tins and sewing needles! Early systems were based on mechanical scanning, but were later replaced by electronic scanning. One of the first major programmes to be publicly transmitted was the coronation procession of George VI in 1936.

First successful cloning of an adult animal

1996
Sheep

Dolly the sheep was created by scientists at the Roslin Institute, Edinburgh. She was made by taking a single cell from an adult sheep's udder. The genetic information from the cell was implanted in an unfertilized egg from which all the original genetic material had been removed. The embryo was then implanted in the womb of a surrogate mother. The resulting lamb was born in 1996 and in

February 1997 the Roslin scientists presented the adult Dolly to the world. Dolly is identical to the adult sheep from which the cell was taken. In April 1998 Dolly gave birth by natural means. Bonnie the lamb is therefore not a clone of her mother.

Energy

Largest oilfield
Al-Ghawar, Saudi Arabia
82 billion barrels (estimated)*

Saudi Arabia has the largest oil reserves in the world (estimated 260 billion barrels). Oil is a fossil fuel, an organic material produced by living organisms. Fossil fuels, such as oil, bitumen, natural gas, and coal, are non-renewable sources of energy, yet provide over 80 per cent of our current energy needs. It is now thought that only some 23 per cent of recoverable deposits of oil remain.

Longest oil pipeline
Trans-Alaskan pipeline
800 miles (1287 km)

The Trans-Alaskan pipeline runs from Prudhoe Bay on the north coast of Alaska to the ice-free port of Valdez, from where the oil is taken by tankers to ports on the west coast of the United States. The pipeline crosses three mountain ranges, 250 watercourses and, for almost half the way, is suspended above the frozen ground. Elsewhere, the pipeline is laid under the permanently frozen ground, and insulated to prevent any thawing of permafrost which would greatly alter the environment. The Trans-Alaskan pipeline cost $9

*One barrel of oil = 35 gallons (159 litres)

billion to construct, carries 1.5 million barrels of oil a day and was completed in 1977.

Largest natural gas deposits
Urengoy, Siberia, Russia
285,000,000,000,000 ft³ (8,087,000,000,000 m³)

Urengoy lies on the Gulf of Ob in west Siberia on the Arctic Circle. There are 15 separate reservoirs of gas in the field and production began in 1978. Like oil, natural gas is a non-renewable fossil fuel, derived from plants and water-borne organic material.

Longest natural gas pipeline
Trans-Siberian pipeline
3,750 miles (6034 km)

The Trans-Siberian pipeline links the huge Siberian gas fields with western Europe, crossing over more than 700 rivers and streams on its way. Natural gas was discovered in Europe in the 17th century, but transporting it proved to be very difficult and limited its use. In 1890 the invention of leakproof pipe coupling was a major breakthrough, but it still could not be transported more than 100 miles (161 km) from its source. The 20th century saw greater advances in technology, and by the 1970s pipes could safely cross huge distances.

Largest dam (by height)
Rogun, Tajikistan
1099 ft (355 m)

Both Syncrude Tailings (above) and Rogun dams are earth and rock-fill (embankment) dams. Earth-fill dams are used to hold back water across broad rivers, partly because huge amounts of material are needed and earth and rocks are more readily available and cheaper than manufactured materials, and partly because earth and rockfill dams will respond to movements below the surface and are therefore less likely to be damaged.

Largest dam (by size of reservoir)
Owen Falls, Uganda
9,540,000,000 ft³ (2,700,000,000 m³)

Owen Falls Dam is on the Victoria Nile and is a gravity dam. Gravity dams use the downward pressure of the weight of the concrete construction materials to resist the horizontal force of the water behind the barrier.

Largest dam (by power capacity)
Turukhansk, Russia
20,000 megawatts

Turukhansk Dam is on the Lower Tunguska river

and is a combined earth-fill and gravity dam, with a concrete base. Hydro-electric power stations such as this convert the power of falling water into electrical energy. Generally, huge amounts of water rush through a tunnel or pipe to a water turbine, where its force causes the turbine shaft to spin. This, in turn, drives an electric generator. Unlike fossil fuels, water is a renewable source of power; it costs less to produce and there is little pollution. Hydro-electric power stations can, however, affect the environment adversely, as experience with Itaipú on the Brazil-Paraguay border has shown. The construction of this large power plant (generating up to 12,600 megawatts) involved the submergence of the once-spectacular Guaíra Falls, and the impact of the various structures which ensure sufficient water flows into the dam have had major detrimental influences on the upstream aquatic environment.

Largest reservoir
Bratsk (Bratskoye), Russia
410 ft (125 m) high, 14,488 ft (4,416 m) at widest, 137,230,000 acre ft (169,300,000,000m^3) reservoir capacity

Bratsk is a large hydro-electric power station with a power capacity of 4,500 megawatts. It was completed in 1964 and its very existence is a tribute to both the designers and the men who constructed it. The conditions in this remote and isolated area meant that men were working in temperatures as low as -72° F (-58° C) for considerable periods of time, with frost on over 280 days of the year. A large aluminium factory and a timber processing plant have since been established in Bratsk to take advantage of the power generated by the dam.

First major tidal power station
Rance, France (1966)

The Rance power station was completed in 1966. It measures 0.5 miles (804 m) across and has 24 tunnels; seawater flows through each tunnel and activates a 10 megawatt turbine. Reversible blades drive the dynamos in the turbines through each ebb and flow of the tide, producing electricity. Tidal power is generated by the energy of the sea waves and can average about 90 kilowatts for every 3.3 ft (1 m) of wave length. Rance power station is the world's first fully-operational system and is linked to France's national electric grid. One year after its opening, it was producing 500,000 kilowatts of electricity. The Brittany coast is particularly suitable for tidal power as it has one of the greatest tidal movements in the world: height differences between waves at high and low tides can be up to 44.3 ft (13.5 m) and waves can reach speeds as high as 55.89 mph (90 kph). Tidal power remains an attractive option for future needs because of its low impact on the environment, but much more research needs to be done for it to become a truly viable option for the 21st century.

Largest water pipeline
13 ft (4 m) diameter
Great Man-Made River Project, Libya, Africa

The Great Man-Made River Project (GMR) is designed to bring high-quality water, for both human and agricultural purposes, from sources deep under the Sahara desert to settlements along the Libyan coast. It was begun in 1983, but will not be complete until 2007. The first stage, GMR1, included collecting water from hundreds of wells and tapping into underground reservoirs. This water was then transported through the pipes to a reservoir at Ajdabiya. These huge pipes are capable of carrying some 70.6 million ft^3 (1,970,680 m^3) a day. The construction of the second pipeline, GMR2, was begun in September 1996 and is intended to supply Libya's capital, Tripoli, with water. When the project is finished, the pipeline will carry some 88 million ft^3 (2,464,000 m^3) of water each day.

First wind-powered generator
Denmark 1890

In 1890, Danish scientist P. Lacour devised a windmill using sails and twin fantails on a steel tower to produce electricity, and thus initiated a 30-year programme of reseach and development in his country. Over 100 machines were soon brought into operation, but in spite of early enthusiasm, wind power still only produces about 1 per cent of Denmark's total electricity requirements. In the first half of the 20th century, hundreds of one kilowatt machines were built for farms and remote communities, mainly the propeller wind turbine type, first used in the Crimea in 1931, but little headway was made in adapting the turbines for mass production. The 1970s oil crisis spurred on attempts to find an alternative to oil and several advanced aerodynamic designs have been produced in the 1980s and 1990s. The largest of these, a wind turbine with two blades, each 160 ft (49 m) long attached to a very high tower, is found on Hawaii. Large wind farms, clusters of wind turbines in an area where a steady wind can be relied upon, are found in Hawaii and California, where some 15,000 turbines are now in operation. Capacities range from 10 to 500 kilowatts per unit. Wind power today is one of the world's fastest-growing energy resources; it is renewable energy and non-polluting (except for visual or aesthetic pollution). Already wind turbines generating a total capacity of over 6000 megawatts have been built and this figure is expected to more than double by the beginning of the year 2000. In Europe alone, wind energy projects produce enough electricity to meet the domestic needs of five million people, and the industry hopes to increase this to 50 million people by 2010. Wind power is also seen as a relatively cheap and accessible form of power for some developing countries.

Largest artificial lake
Lake Victoria (Victoria Nyanza), Africa
26,418 miles² (68,422 km²)

Lake Victoria borders Kenya, Tanzania and Uganda. It is 210 miles (338 km) long and 150 miles (241 km) at its widest. The chief tributary is the Kagera river and the flow of water is controlled by the Owen Falls Dam in Uganda (see Largest dam (by size of reservoir) above). Lake Victoria was named in honour of Queen Victoria by John H. Speke in 1858, the first European explorer to find it. The level of the natural lake was raised by some 3 ft (0.91 m) when the Owen Falls Dam was constructed in 1954, thus turning it technically into an artificial lake.

Largest artificial island
Flevoland Polders, Netherlands
551 miles² (1427 km²) area

The two Flevoland Polders (land reclaimed from the sea) form a continuous land area and are joined to the rest of the Netherlands by dikes, bridges and causeways. The land was reclaimed during the 1950s and 1960s, and in 1986 the new Dutch province of Flevoland was created. The polders were originally intended to be used mainly for agriculture (reclaimed land is usually very fertile), but instead they have become very popular for residential, recreational and industrial purposes. The principal cities are Lelystad and Almere, and the population is about 250,000. One quarter of Flevoland lies below sea level and the coasts are protected by dikes and sand dunes. The most important dike is that enclosing the Zuiderzee (Shallow Sea), which is 18 miles (30 km) long, thus turning it technically into a lake, the Ijsselmeer. If it were not for the dikes, over two-fifths of the land would be almost permanently flooded, and pumps work continually to keep the sea at bay.

Largest tidal river barrier
Oosterschelde Dam, Netherlands
5 miles (8 km)

The Oosterschelde (Eastern Schelde) Dam stretches across the Oosterschelde estuary in the southwest Netherlands. It represents a vital part of the Delta Plan to close the sea inlets of the southwestern delta, mainly in the province of Zeeland. This became a matter of national priority after the disastrous gales and spring tides of 1 February 1953 which combined to flood up to 400,000 acres (162,000 hectares) and killed almost 2000 people. Some 10 dams and two bridges were built between 1960 and 1987, the largest being the Oosterschelde Dam, a storm-surge barrier with 61 openings that can be closed when necessary. The openings are generally left open to allow sea water to flow naturally into the estuary, thus limiting damage to the environment.

Building and Construction

Largest government office complex
Pentagon, Arlington County, Virginia, USA
34 acres (13.77 hectares)

Designed by George Bergstrom, the Pentagon was constructed in 1941–43. It is made up of five concentric pentagons or five-sided buildings, with connecting corridors. Each has five floors plus mezzanine and basement. The Pentagon is the headquarters of the United States Defense departments of the army, navy and air force, and the office accommodation is supplemented by a shopping precinct and car parks, together with bus, train and taxi stations and a heliport.

Largest commercial office complex
World Trade Center, New York, USA
12 million ft^2 (1,116,000 m^2) usable floor space

The twin towers of this complex of six buildings rise to some 1350 ft (411 m) and 110 storeys. The World Trade Center was built by the New York and New Jersey Port Authority as a focus for both government and commercial agencies involved in international trade. On 26 February 1993, a massive terrorist bomb was detonated in the underground garage, causing several deaths as well as considerable damage to the building.

Tallest office building
Petronas Towers, Kuala Lumpur, Malaysia (1995)
1476 ft (450 m)

Tallest office building in the UK
Canary Wharf, London (1990)
800 ft (244 m)

Tallest office building in North America
Sears Tower, Chicago, USA (1974)
1453 ft (443 m)

First passenger lift
Haughwort Department Store, New York City, USA (1857)

The first safe passenger lift to come into use was installed by Elisha Otis. Without lifts, high-rise buildings would never have been practicable – no-one would willingly live or work more than four or five storeys high. In 1889 Eiffel installed hydraulic lifts in his tower in Paris.

Tallest monument
Gateway to the West Arch, St Louis, Missouri, USA
625 ft (190 m)

The arch was designed by Eero Saarinen and erected in 1965 as a celebration of the city's role as a starting point for westward expansion in the 19th century.

Largest cathedral
St John the Divine, New York City, USA
Begun in 1892, this neo-Gothic cathedral has the longest nave in the world.

Largest cathedral in the UK
Cathedral Church of Christ, Liverpool, England
This Anglican, neo-Gothic cathedral was begun in 1903, but not consecrated until 1978. The central tower rises to some 330 ft (100.6 m).

Largest tomb
Mount Li, near Xi'an, China
Mount Li was discovered by archaeologists in 1974. It is the burial place of Qin Shihuangdi and dates from the Qin (Ch'in) dynasty. Qin Shihuangdi ruled 221–210 BC and first united China, establishing standards for the law, monetary and road systems, weights and measures and written language. The great emperor's body is 'guarded' by 7000 lifesize

warriors, all individually moulded and complete
with their crossbows, spears and horses.

Highest church spire
*Ulm Cathedral, Baden-Württemberg,
Germany*
528 ft (161 m)

> The Protestant Gothic cathedral was begun in 1377
> but not finished until 1890.

Highest church spire in the UK
Salisbury Cathedral, Wiltshire, England
404 ft (123 m)

> The cathedral was begun in 1220 and remains one
> of the finest in Europe.

Tallest tower
KTHI-TV tower, North Dakota, USA
2064 ft (629 m)

Tallest tower in Europe
Ostankino TV tower, Moscow, Russia
1762 ft (537 m)

Longest wall
Great Wall of China
4000 miles (6437 km) (including branches)

The Great Wall of China was built by Emperor Qin Shihuangdi (see above, Largest tomb) in the 3rd century BC to prevent the Huns from attacking and harassing his lands in northern China. It was extended and rebuilt by later Chinese dynasties and stretches from the Yellow Sea to central Asia.

Longest artificial waterway
Grand Canal, Changzhou–Beijing, China
994 miles (1600 km)

The construction of the Grand Canal is believed to have begun before the birth of Christ. the northern section was built in the 1200s and the canal is still in use today. The Chinese were the first people to design and build canal locks.

Longest artificial waterway in Europe
Volga–Baltic Waterway, Russia
229 miles (368 km)

The Volga–Baltic Waterway runs from Rybinsk to the Gulf of Finland on the Baltic Sea. It is a system of canalized rivers and man-made canals and was completed in 1964. There are a total of seven automatic locks along the route and the waterway connects with the White Sea–Baltic canal at Lake Onega.

Longest artificial waterway in North America
St Lawrence Seaway, Canada/USA
182 miles (293 km)

The St Lawrence Seaway was built jointly by the USA and Canada and completed in 1959. Using rivers, lakes and canals, the Seaway links the Atlantic Ocean with the Great Lakes. There are seven large locks along the route.

Longest artificial waterway in South America
Panama Canal, Central America
50 miles (80 km)

The Panama Canal cuts across the Isthmus of Panama and links the Atlantic and Pacific Oceans. It was constructed by the United States and took 10 years and millions of dollars to build. Thousands of labourers forced their way through jungles and swamps, fighting disease and wild animals, to construct the canal which was completed in 1914.

The Canal shortens shipping journeys from the east coast of America to the west coast by thousands of miles; before it was constructed, ships had to go right round South America. There are 12 locks on the Canal.

Longest artificial waterway in Africa
Suez Canal, Egypt
100 miles (161 km)

The Suez Canal runs from Port Said, Egypt, to the Gulf of Suez and links the Red Sea and the Mediterranean. It shortens the route for ships between Europe and the Persian Gulf, India, Australia and the Far East. In 1853 the great French engineer, Ferdinand de Lesseps, obtained permission from the Egyptians to construct the canal, but work was not begun until six years later. It was finished in 1869 but has been enlarged and expanded over the years as ships have increased in size. There are no locks in the Suez Canal.

Longest artificial waterway in Asia
Grand Canal, Changzhou–Beijing, China
994 miles (1600 km)

See Longest artificial waterway, p.192.

Longest bridge
Lake Pontchartrain Causeway (No. 2)
23.9 miles (38.5 km)

The twin causeways of Lake Pontchartrain shorten the travelling distance between New Orleans and Mandeville, Louisiana, USA. No. 1 Causeway was completed in 1956 and No. 2 in 1969. Both are made of pre-cast, pre-stressed concrete and are multispan.

Longest suspension bridge (main span)
Akashi Kaikyo, Hyogo, Japan
6529 ft (1990 m)

This bridge links Kobe on the island of Honshu to Awaji island and is part of an ongoing project to build 17 bridges which will ultimately connect Honshu to the island of Shikoku. In suspension bridges, the central road/railway hangs from steel cables which are supported by two high towers. The towers themselves are supported by steel spans which stretch between each tower and its anchorage on the bank; anchorages can be huge concrete blocks or bedrock. Suspension bridges can be used in difficult terrain, to cross deep water or gorges, because they need only two towers. On the other hand, they can be unstable in high winds.

Longest suspension bridge in Europe (main span)

Store Baelt (Great Belt, East Belt), Zeeland–Funen, Denmark (1997)
5328 ft (1624 m)

Longest suspension bridge in the UK (main span)

Humber Estuary, Yorkshire/Lincolnshire, England (1981)
4626 ft (1410 m)

Longest suspension bridge in North America (main span)

Verrazano Narrows, New York City, USA (1964)
4258 ft (1298 m)

Longest cantilever bridge

Quebec Bridge, Quebec, Canada
Main span 1801 ft (549 m); total length 3238 ft (987 m)

The Quebec Bridge spans the St Laurence river

between Ste Foy and St Nicolas, Quebec. It was completed in 1917. Cantilever bridges have two beams or cantilevers extending from a pier or tower on each bank. These two beams, which support the roadway, are connected by a third, central section. Supporting girders often form a typical flattened diamond shape around the central road or railway.

Longest steel arch bridge
New River Gorge, New River, near Fayetteville, West Virginia, USA (1977)
Main span 1699 ft (518 m)

First known tunnel
Babylon (Iraq) 22nd century BC
The first known tunnel was about 11 ft (3.4 m) high and of arched brickwork design. It ran under the river Euphrates, connecting a temple and a royal palace.

Longest undersea tunnel
Channel Tunnel, linking Kent, England to Calais, France (1994)
$32^1/_4$ miles (51.8 km)

Longest road tunnel
St Gotthard, Göschenen to Airlo,
Switzerland (1980)
10 miles (16.1 km)

Longest railway tunnel
Seikan Tunnel, linking islands of Honshu
and Hokkaido, Japan (1988)
$33^1/_2$ miles (53.8 km)

Longest underground railway tunnel
Moscow, Belyaevo to Medvedkovo
19 miles (30.6 km)

Widest tunnel
Antwerp, Belgium
187 ft (57 m)

> The tunnel runs under the river Scheldt; it has eight
> road and railway lanes, plus routes for cyclists and
> motorcyclists.

Longest water tunnel
Delaware Aqueduct, New York City, USA
105 miles (168 km)

The water tunnel penetrates to depths as great as 2500 ft (762 m) below ground. It was built between 1937 and 1953.

Largest aqueduct system
California, 685 miles (1102 km)

An aqueduct is a man-made channel designed to carry water to where it is needed. Aqueducts have been constructed since ancient times and it is known that the Greeks used them. The Romans supplied Rome with water through the use of aqueducts, and went on to build them in cities throughout the Roman Empire. Nowadays aqueducts have been largely supplanted by waterpipes, but they are still used where appropriate. The California project has been operational since 1960 and is part of a major plan to redirect water from the northern part of the state as far as the Mexican border, for both domestic and agricultural uses.

Largest sports stadium
Strahov Stadium, Prague, Czech Republic
240,000 spectators

The Strahov Stadium was built in 1934 for the Sokol gymnastics exhibition.

First fully-roofed sports stadium
Astrodome, Houston, Texas, USA
62,000 spectators

The Astrodome, the first fully-roofed, air-conditioned stadium in the world, was constructed in 1965. The roof spans 642 ft (196 m), is made of transparent plastic panels supported by steel beams, and rises to 208 ft (63.4 m) above the field. The temperature is kept at a steady 74 °F (23 °C).

First self-service grocers
Memphis, Tennessee, USA (1916)

Largest shopping centre
West Edmonton Mall, Alberta, Canada

The West Edmonton Mall offers shoppers over 800 stores, restaurants, hotel, funfair, church, lake, sunbathing and surfing opportunities, zoo and landscaped grounds planted with trees. It was opened in 1981.

Largest shopping centre in Europe
MetroCentre, Gateshead, Tyne and Wear, England

The MetroCentre offers over 350 shops, restaurants, cinema and leisure facilities.

Largest port
Port of New York and New Jersey, New York, USA
751 miles (1208 km) navigable waters

The Port of New York Authority controls all the waterways and port facilities within 25 miles of the Statue of Liberty. There are over 250 berths for large ships and the port handles over 100 million tons of cargo each year.

Busiest port
Rotterdam–Europoort, Netherlands

Rotterdam was heavily bombed in World War II (1939–45) and rebuilding work included a completely new port. Rotterdam handles millions of tons of cargo each year, especially oil, petroleum and grain. Its position at the mouth of the rivers Meuse and Rhine means that, in addition to large tankers and other sea-going ships, Rotterdam can also handle many thousands of cargo-carrying river barges.

Busiest airport
Heathrow Airport, London, England
54.5 million passengers per annum

Largest railway station
Grand Central Terminal, New York City, USA

48 acres (19.4 hectares)

The station was constructed by the American millionaire Cornelius Vanderbilt (1794–1877). He had already bought the railway lines from New York to Chicago, thus offering passengers the first direct service between the two cities, and the station was to be the New York terminal for the journey. The construction of the building gave much-needed work to many thousands of unemployed people in a period of economic depression. The station has 44 platforms.

Largest railway station in the UK
Waterloo, London

30 acres (12.2 hectares)

Waterloo Station has recently been expanded to provide facilities for trains using the Channel Tunnel.

First theme park
Disneyland, Anaheim, California, USA (1955)

Largest theme park
Disney World, Orlando, Florida, USA (1971)

Largest theme park in Europe
Euro Disneyland, Marne-la-Vallée, near Paris, France (1992)

First known lighthouse
Pharos of Alexandria, (c. 270 BC)

The Pharos stood at the entrance to the harbour at Alexandria in Egypt. It stood some 450 ft (135 m) high and its light could be seen some 40 miles (65 km) away. It is now considered to be one of the Seven Wonders of the Ancient World, but was in ruins by the 15th century.

Only survivor of the Seven Wonders of the Ancient World
Egyptian pyramids

The pyramids are thought to have been constructed over 4000 years ago as tombs for the pharoahs (kings) of Egypt. They are the oldest known tombs in the world.

The other Seven Wonders of the World were: the

Statue of Zeus at Olympia; the Mausoleum of Halicarnassus; the Hanging Gardens of Babylon; the Temple of Artemis at Ephesus; the Colossus of Rhodes; and the Pharos of Alexandria (see First known lighthouse, p.203).

Transport

First successful manned balloon flight

21 November 1783, Paris, France

The successful launch and return to earth of the pioneer balloonists, Jean-François Pilâtre de Rozier and François Laurent, Marquis d'Arlandes, who travelled over the Bois de Boulogne at a height of 84 ft (25.6 m), marked the fulfilment of a centuries-old dream, the possibility of flight. The 4 min 2 sec flight was in a balloon designed by the famous Montgolfier brothers, Joseph (1740–1810) and Etienne (1745–99). Some years earlier, the brothers had noticed that when a paper bag was held over a fire, it would inflate and rise up the chimney. Further experimentation led them to replace hot air with hydrogen – fortunately, perhaps, not realizing quite how flammable the gas could be. The possibilities of ballooning were further exploited in the 19th century and the French used balloons for spying on their enemies during the Napoleonic wars; in later conflicts they were used for taking aerial photographs. Hydrogen has long been replaced by the safer helium. Today balloons are used mainly for collecting certain kinds of data for meteorological and leisure purposes. Enthusiasts still try to break the existing records for speed and distance, and world championships take place regularly in various countries, controlled by the FAI, the sport's governing body.

Highest manned balloon flight
113,740 ft (34,668 m)

Commander M.D. Ross of the United States Naval Reserve and his crew broke all records with this achievement in 1961.

First Atlantic crossing by balloon
August 1978

Americans Ben Abruzzo, Maxie Anderson and Larry Newman achieved the first crossing in their helium balloon, *Double Eagle II*. Their flight took 137 hr.

Largest airship
Hindenburg (LZ129)
804 ft (245 m) long, 134 ft 6 in (41 m) wide

The main problem with balloons was that they were not navigable, but this difficulty was resolved with the development of airships. Originally known as zeppelins, after their German creator Ferdinand, Graf von Zeppelin, the first flight of an airship took place in July 1900. The public took to the idea of travelling in these lighter-than-air craft with enthusiasm and, over the next three decades, they became very popular. The travelling section, suspended under the huge, usually cigar-shaped balloon, was often luxuriously equipped and spacious. The giant *Hindenburg*, named after the

German president of the day, was launched on its maiden flight in 1936. Intended for the transatlantic crossing, this rigid airship could travel at speeds of up to 84 mph (135 km/h), powered by four 1000 hp diesel engines, and could accommodate around 90 passengers. On 6 May 1937, while docking at Lakehurst, New Jersey, USA, the *Hindenburg* exploded, killing 35 of its 97 passengers and crew. This terrible accident signalled the end of commercial airship travel.

Longest airship flight
264 hours, March 1957

Led by Commander J.R. Hunt of the United States Navy, the crew of a ZPG-2 class airship travelled non-stop, via Africa and the Cape Verde islands, from Massachusetts to Florida, USA, without refuelling.

Largest passenger aeroplane
Boeing 747
Wingspan 211 ft (64.3 m), up to 500 passengers

The 'jumbo jet' needs only two pilots and can fly over 8000 miles (12,874 km) non-stop at a cruise speed of around 403 mph (648.5 km/h). The Boeing company was founded by the American, William E. Boeing (1881–1956). His first plane was a seaplane, built from sitka spruce (Boeing was a lumber producer in Seattle at the time). During the 1920s and '30s, the Boeing company built military aircraft before merging with other companies to produce several bomber aircraft for use in World War II (1939–45), including the B17 Flying Fortress and B29 Superfortress. The Boeing company produced America's first jet passenger aeroplane, the Boeing 707, in 1958. The 747 began its first regular passenger service in 1970. The Boeing company has also been closely involved with the development of the Apollo and Saturn moon rockets and the Minuteman intercontinental ballistic missile.

Largest aeroplane wingspan
Spruce Goose
319 ft 11 in (97.57 m)

This eight-engined, wooden flying boat made one flight only, piloted by its owner and designer, the American billionaire Howard Hughes. Howard Robard Hughes (1905–76) was born in Houston, Texas and inherited an industrial empire on his father's death. His twin passions were films and flying and he had enough money to indulge them both. In the 1930s and '40s he produced several films, including the notorious *The Outlaw* (1943) and bought RKO Pictures. He was also head of Hughes Aircraft Company and designed and flew several experimental planes, often setting new speed records. In the 1940s he designed the huge *Spruce Goose*, which was to be capable of carrying 700 passengers. Its single flight was over 0.99 miles (1.6 km) at a height of 69 ft 4 in (21 m). The aircraft is now on display at Long Beach, California. Hughes became increasingly eccentric as he grew older and, obsessed with eliminating bacteria and dust from his surroundings, died a total recluse.

First man to break the sound barrier in air
Charles Yeager (1947)

Captain Charles (Chuck) E. Yeager (born 1923) of the United States Air Force, piloted a Bell X-1 rocket plane on 14 October 1947 and became the first man in history to break the sound barrier. He set a further record on 12 December 1953 by flying two and a half times the speed of sound in a Bell X-1A. Yeager retired from the air force after a long and distinguished career, and in 1986 was appointed to the presidential commission investigating the explosion of the space shuttle *Challenger*.

Highest air speed
2193 mph (3529 km/h) July 1976

Captain E.W. Joersz broke all previous records with this flight in a military Lockheed plane, known as the *Blackbird*, and used for surveillance. The speed of sound (Mach 1) is about 761 mph (1225 km/h) at ground level, but it declines in speed with the increase of altitude. When an aeroplane is flying it causes pressure disturbances (differences in air pressure) in the air around it. These disturbances move at the speed of sound so, if the aeroplane is flying at normal speeds, the disturbances move ahead of the aircraft and pose no problems. If the aeroplane is travelling at the speed of sound itself, it is moving as fast as the disturbances, which cannot then get out of the way and build up round the nose and tail of the aircraft as shockwaves, causing vibration and control problems. At supersonic speeds, the build-up of shockwaves is even greater, causing sonic booms (loud, explosive sounds) which can be heard by people on the ground.

Fastest passenger aeroplane
Concorde
Cruising speed up to 1304 mph (2100 km/h)

The BAC/Aérospatiale Concorde, a joint production between France and the UK, was first flown in 1969 and began regular passenger services in 1976. It is the first and, to date the only, supersonic airliner (ie goes faster than the speed of sound), and has flown between London and New York in as little as three hours. Only 16 Concordes have been built. Its distinctive shape, with sharply-pointed nose and swept-back wings, are typical of supersonic aircraft, and represent design solutions to the problems of 'drag' (the aerodynamic force that resists the forward movement of the aeroplane) and excessive stress when the plane flies at supersonic speeds.

Highest aeroplane flight
314,750 ft (95,936 m) 1962

United States Air Force pilot Major Robert M. White flew his X-15 rocket plane so high that he could qualify as a spaceman! The X-15 is capable of flying at speeds in excess of Mach 5 (five times the speed of sound), making it a hypersonic aircraft.

Largest ship
Jahre Viking
1504 ft (458 m) long, 226 ft (68.8 m) wide

This massive oil tanker was built in Japan in 1979. The first ocean-going oil tanker, the little *Glückauf*, was designed and constructed in Britain for her American owners in 1885. Purpose-built to carry oil from the United States to Europe, the *Glückauf* served as a model for the type. It was 295 ft 4 in

(90 m) long and 36 ft (11 m) wide. Oil tankers carry their cargo over long distances economically and efficiently, but their very size makes them unwieldy, and prone to accidents. They also require deep ports for docking.

Longest liner
Norway
1033 ft (315 m)

The *Norway*, formerly known as the *France*, was built in France in 1961. She carries around 1000 crew and 2000 passengers.

Largest liner (passenger capacity)
Sovereign of the Seas
2700 passengers

The *Sovereign of the Seas* was built in Norway in 1988 and carries 750 crew.

Fastest speed on water
275 knots (316$^1/_2$ mph/509 km/h)

The record was set in October 1978 by Kenneth Warby in a hydroplane, *The Spirit of Australia*, in New South Wales, Australia. Hydroplanes, with their specially-shaped hulls which skim or 'plane' over the surface of the water, are designed for speed. The flat or slightly curved bottom of the hydroplane allows water pressure to build up, lifting and keeping the boat on the surface of the water, and thus allowing it to go faster.

Fastest Atlantic crossing
2 days 10 hr 34 min 47 sec

The record was achieved by the crew of the speedboat *Destriero* in August 1992.

First hovercraft
SR.NI (1959)

The SR.NI hovercraft was designed and built in Britain in 1959, although the idea was first explored by Sir John Thorneycroft in the 1870s. Thorneycroft conceived of an amphibious machine, with its weight supported by a cushion of air between the craft and the ground or water beneath, but he could not solve the problem of how to keep the cushion of air from escaping from underneath the craft. It was not until the 1950s that Sir Christopher Cockerell solved this problem and constructed the first working model – which carried three passengers and could only operate slowly over calm water or even ground. Enthusiasm for the hovercraft was high in the 1960s with designers and manufacturers optimistically envisaging ocean-going hovercraft in the near future. As it is, Britain is the only country which uses hovercraft on a commercial scale. Cross-channel hovercraft are fast and can take around 400 passengers and 50 vehicles. Hovercraft also have military uses.

Fastest commercial hovercraft
SR.N4
Up to 70 mph (112.7 km/h)

These cross-channel hovercraft, which run between England and France, are also the largest in regular commercial use. They can accommodate up to 418 passengers and 60 vehicles.

First nuclear-powered merchant ship
Savannah (1959)

The 593 ft 9 in (181 m) long *Savannah* was built in the USA two years after the world's first nuclear-powered ship, the Soviet Union ice-breaker *Lenin* came into service. Named after the first steamship to cross the Atlantic, the *Savannah* cruised around the world carrying both passengers and cargo. But the huge cost of building the ship, together with the high running costs (she required twice the number of crew members and cargo space was limited because of the need to insulate the nuclear core), made the ship commercially impractical. The *Savannah* was taken out of service in 1971 after only 12 years.

Fastest steam engine
Mallard
$125^1/_2$ mph (202 km/h)

This British streamline LNER A4 class locomotive achieved the world record in 1938. It has never been beaten.

Fastest electric train
L'Atlantique TGV
320 mph (515 km/h)

The French TGV (Train à Grande Vitesse, high-speed train), the pride of SNCF railways, still holds the official record (dating from 1991), despite stiff competition, especially from Japan. In December 1997, a prototype manned Japanese maglev (magnetically levitated) train hurtled along on a test run at 332 mph (534.1 km/h).

Fastest diesel engine in regular service
Intercity 125
162 mph (261 km/h)

The British Intercity 125 locomotive is certainly

capable of reaching these speeds, but its average speed on the London to Edinburgh run was a slightly less breathtaking 95 mph (153 km/h) before being replaced by electric engines.

Fastest regular passenger service
100 mph (160 km/h) Tokaido Line, Japan

The Tokaido line runs between Tokyo and Osaka. The streamlined electric Hikari trains leave both terminal cities four times an hour and complete the 320 mile (515 km) journey in just over three hours.

Highest railway line
Central Railway, Peru
Up to 19,685 ft (6000 m) above sea level

The railway runs between Peru and Bolivia and crosses the Andes mountains. It is used mainly for freight, carrying the minerals which are mined there. The problems of such enormous heights and steep gradients are solved by utilizing curves, tunnels and toothed rack sections.

Highest railway station
Condor, Bolivia
15,705 ft (4787 m)

Longest rail journey
Moscow to Vladivostok, Russia
5786 miles (9311 km), approx 8 days

The Trans-Siberian railway was begun in 1891, but not finished until 1915. Russia has the highest passenger railway usage in Europe.

Longest stretch of straight rail track
Nullarbor Plain, Western Australia
296³/₄ miles (478 km)

This track forms part of the railway line which stretches across Australia from Perth on the west to Sydney on the east. The journey, on the 'Indian Pacific' train, is a total of 2445¹/₂ miles (3938 km) and lasts for three days.

First underground system
London Underground (1863)

The first underground trains ran between Paddington and Farringdon stations and used coal-burning steam engines. The air extraction system failed to keep the tunnels clean, but despite the fumes the system proved popular. Other cities followed suit, including Glasgow, Budapest, Paris and New York. The underground in Moscow was begun in 1932 and carries around 6.5 million passengers each day, more than any other system.

First mass-produced car
Oldsmobile, USA (1901)

Eli Ransom Olds (1864–1950) designed and manufactured the 3 hp Oldsmobile, the first commercially successful American car, and the first to be made using an assembly-line system. The first Oldsmobiles were marketed in 1901 and by 1904 sales reached an astonishing 5000. In 1905 Olds had a disagreement with his wealthy backer, Samuel L. Smith, left the Olds Motor Works and began his own company, the Reo Motor Car Company. The company enjoyed great success at first, but soon declined, and Olds turned his attention to other interests, including the invention of a lawnmower.

Longest car
Bugatti Type 41 (Golden Bugatti or La Royale)
22 ft (6.7 m)

Ettore Bugatti (1881-1947) was born in Milan, Italy. He began to build luxury and racing cars in Alsace in 1909, and in the 1920s produced the Royale, probably one of the most luxurious and meticulously constructed cars of all time. It was certainly one of the most expensive and only a handful (6–8) were ever completed. Bugatti died in

Paris in 1947 and the famous cars died with him,
the company failing quickly after his death.

Best-selling car
Volkswagen Beetle
Over 21 million sold

The Volkswagen ('people's car') company was
founded in 1937 by the German government to
produce a low-priced car for ordinary people.
Controlled by the German Labour Front, a Nazi
organization, the company recruited Ferdinand
Porsche to design it. The city of Wolfsburg was
chosen for the Volkswagen factory, but both city
and factory were destroyed during World War II
(1939–45). After the war, the Allies encouraged the
resurgence of the German car industry, centring on
the Volkswagen company. The car was first named
the Beetle, because of its distinctive, rounded
appearance, by an American advertising company.
The design remained virtually the same until
production ceased in the mid-1990s; however, a
newer, more up-to-date model is now being
developed.

Fastest speed on land
763 mph (1228 km/h)

Andy Green, a British airforce pilot, achieved this

record on 15 October 1997 in Black Rock Desert, Nevada, USA. Green actually broke the sound barrier twice in his jet car, *Thrust SSC*, averaging 763 mph (1228 km/h), which is above the speed of sound under local conditions. The first run was made two days earlier, but was not officially recognized because Green failed to complete two separate runs within an hour as required – he took 61 min to complete his two runs. The second attempt, on 15 October, puts him in the record books for a feat which many people thought could never be achieved.

Fastest production car
Lamborghini Diablo SV
190+ mph (305.8+ km/h)

The Lamborghini Diablo accelerates from 0–60 mph (0–96.56 km/h) in 3.8 sec and costs £136,000.

Fastest production motorbike
V & M Honda Blackbird
200 mph (322 km/h)

Largest bicycle
Frankencycle
73 ft (22.24 m) long, 10 ft (3.05 m) wheel diameter

The *Frankencycle* was built in California in 1988 and ridden by four men for a distance of 807 ft (246 m).

Country with highest number of bicycles
China
300 million (estimated)

Highest road
18,000 ft (5486.4 m) above sea level

This road lies on the borders of Tibet and China in the Himalayas.

Lowest road
1290 ft (393 m) below sea level.

The road runs along the shores of the Dead Sea in Israel.

Longest road
Pan-American Highway
30,000 miles (48,000 km) total length

The Pan-American Highway runs from Alaska to Chile, with connecting routes extending to Paraguay, Argentina and Brazil. The road links the east and west coasts of South America and includes the capitals of 17 countries along the way. It was originally designed to be a single highway, but it now includes many feeder routes, which connect it to previously remote and isolated places. Once out of the United States, the landscape varies from dense jungles to remote mountains, and the spectacular scenery is home to all kinds of wildlife.

Country with the densest network of roads
Belgium
Approx 2600 miles (4200 km) of road to every 621 miles^2 (1000 km^2) of land.

Widest street
426 ft (130 m)
Avenida 9 de Julio, Buenos Aires, Argentina

Biggest city square
Tiananmen Square, Beijing, China
100 acres (40.5 hectares)

The square was originally laid in 1651 and subsequently enlarged several times. Its name is derived from the Tiananmen gate (Gate of Heavenly Peace), which led into the former Imperial Palace at one end of the square. The flagged square is lined with museums and other public buildings, including the Great Hall of the

People, the venue for the annual meeting of the National People's Congress. In June 1989, a massive pro-democracy student demonstration in the square was forcibly put down by the army. Estimates of the number killed by troops range from several hundred to many thousands, and the true figure will probably never be known. Subsequently, Tiananmen Square has become a symbol of Chinese Communist repression.

First traffic lights
London, England (1868)

The first traffic lights were manually operated and gas-lit; the revolving lantern stood on a pillar near the Houses of Parliament in London and its sole purpose was to allow MPs easier access in and out of the Palace of Westminster.

First electric traffic lights
Cleveland, Ohio, USA (1914)

First parking meter
Oklahoma City, Oklahoma, USA (1935)

First traffic wardens
New York City, USA (1960)

Arts and
Entertainment

First film shown to a paying audience
Paris (1895)

The two Lumière brothers, Auguste (1862–1954) and Louis (1864–1948), invented the cinématographe, a hand-operated combined camera and projector, enabling the first moving films to be shown. On 28 December 1895 the brothers showed 12 short films to an audience, at a ticket price of 1 franc, in the Grand Café in Paris. The screening lasted half an hour and included *Watering the Gardener*, a humorous anecdote involving a garden hose and a small boy, and *Arrival of a Train at Ciotat Station* (running time just under a minute), during which a train is seen rushing headlong towards the audience – causing several terrified customers to make for the exits!

First successful feature film
The Great Train Robbery (1903)

The Great Train Robbery, edited by Edward S. Porter, was the cinema's first major box office success and also the first Western film. The film lasted 12 minutes and helped to establish the telling of realistic stories as the cinema's dominant form. This contrasted with the earlier development of fantasy films, such as Georges Mélié's extraordinary *Trip to the Moon* (1902).

First female film director
Alice Guy (1906)

Alice Guy was the supervising director for Gaumont Pictures, founded by Léon Gaumont in 1895. This French company manufactured equipment and mass-produced films from its studios at La Villette from 1905–14. They were the largest film studios in the world at that time.

First spectacular silent feature film
Quo Vadis? (1912)

Quo Vadis? (*Who Goes There?*) was the prototype for the lavish film spectacular. A story of the Roman Empire, the film was made by the Italian Cines Company and involved the building of huge three-dimensional sets representing Rome, and the hiring of 5000 extras. The success of the film encouraged ever more extravagance and Italia Company's 1914 epic, *Cabiria*, a tale of the Second Punic War (218–201 BC), included the burning of the Roman fleet, Hannibal and his elephants crossing the Alps, and the destruction of the city of Carthage. Such films whetted the public's appetite for spectacle and without them the later great epics of D.W. Griffith and Cecil B. deMille might never have been conceived.

Most expensive silent film
Ben Hur (1925)

MGM's *Ben Hur* was taken from a novel by General Lew Wallace, published in 1880. The filming involved removing the entire company on location from the USA to Italy. Beset by production problems (the original director, star and writer were all dismissed), the production head, Irvine Thalberg, ordered the whole company back to America after the filming of a sea battle, during which it was discovered that most of the Italian extras, playing sailors on the sinking ships, could not swim. Unfortunately, even when filming continued on home ground, the problems continued and the final cost was just under $4 million. The film was very popular, enjoyed great prestige but made little profit.

First sound film
The Jazz Singer (1927)

The film was not a sound film as it is generally understood today, but included some scenes with Al Jolson, the star, singing and speaking with synchronized sound. The sound was recorded on a disc, then synchronized with the film strip. This cumbersome method was soon replaced by an electronic system which recorded sound directly on to the film strip. *The Jazz Singer* was, however, a major breakthrough in film, although some film experts and critics predicted that sound 'would never catch on' with the film-going public!

First animated cartoon film
Humorous Phases of Funny Faces (1906)

The maker of *Humorous Phases* was James Stewart Blackton, an American newspaper illustrator. His animated film centred on drawings of funny faces on a blackboard, and was filmed frame by frame.

First full-length animated feature film
Snow White and the Seven Dwarfs (1937)

Walt Disney (1901–66) is probably the most famous name in cinema history. Disney began his career as a commercial artist in Kansas City, USA, where he soon developed an interest in making animated commercials, followed by short cartoons which he called *Laugh-o-grams*. In 1923 Disney went to Hollywood where he was soon producing live-action cartoons, such as *Alice in Cartoonland*. *Oswald the Rabbit* (1927) was followed by the first appearance of Mickey Mouse, initially in two silent animations, then in *Steamboat Willie* (1925). From then on, Walt Disney never looked back; an astute businessman, he created a vast merchandising operation to exploit the characters he created, and

Walt Disney Studios became renowned the world over. Animated cartoons need 24 separate pictures to represent just one second of screen movement, and *Snow White* is estimated to contain over 450,000 individual drawings. The film was shown all over the world, and dubbed into 13 languages.

First major film festival
Venice, Italy (1932)

First 'Smell-o-Vision' film
The Scent of Mystery (USA, 1959)

Advertised with the slogan 'First they moved, then they talked, now they smell!'; it was not a success.

Largest film set
55 acres (22 hectares)

The Roman forum in *The Fall of the Roman Empire* (USA, 1964).

Most extras
300,000 Gandhi (GB, 1982)

Most expensive film
Titanic (USA, 1997) £200 million

Most money made from one film
Titanic (USA, 1997) £575 million

Greatest loss ever made from one film
Cutthroat Island (USA, 1995) £58,700,000

Country with largest film output
India

The Indian film industry produces around 750 films a year.

European country with largest film output
France

The French film industry produces around 140 films a year.

First Oscar awards
1928

Best Picture: *Wings*; Best Director: Frank Borzage and Lewis Milestone; Best Actress: Janet Gaynor; Best Actor: Emil Jannings.

The 'Oscars' are awarded by the Academy of Motion Picture Arts and Sciences, which initiated

the awards in 1927 to improve the quality and
prestige of film-making. The Oscar statuette is a
gold-plated nude male figure standing on a reel of
film punched with five holes, each representing a
branch of film-making. Legend has it that a
librarian at the Academy commented that the
statuette looked like her Uncle Oscar and so it was
named.

Film with most Oscar awards
*11 Ben Hur (USA, 1959), Titanic (USA,
1997)*

Ben Hur was nominated in 12 categories. *Titanic*
was nominated in 14 categories (see Film with most
Oscar nominations below).

Film with most Oscar nominations
*14 All About Eve (USA, 1950), Titanic
(USA, 1997)*

All About Eve was awarded six Oscars. *Titanic* was
awarded 11 Oscars, equalling *Ben Hur's* hitherto
unbroken record (see above).

Most Oscar awards
29 Walt Disney Studios

Most Oscar-nominated actor never to win an award

7 Richard Burton

Most Best Actress awards

4 Katharine Hepburn

Katharine Hepburn was nominated 12 times for the Best Actress award and is the only actress to have won in consecutive years, 1967 and 1968.

Most Best Actor awards

2 Spencer Tracy, Fredric March, Gary Cooper, Marlon Brando, Dustin Hoffman, Tom Hanks, Jack Nicholson

Longest theatrical run

The Mousetrap

Agatha Christie's *The Mousetrap* opened at the Ambassadors Theatre in London on 25 November 1952 and ran there for 8,862 performances over the next 21 years, the longest continuous run for any play at one theatre. *The Mousetrap* transferred to St Martin's Theatre and is still running, having now achieved over 19,000 performances.

Longest-running musical
Cats

Andrew Lloyd-Webber's *Cats* is based on T.S. Eliot's poems from his *Old Possum's Book of Practical Cats*. In September 1991, Andrew Lloyd Webber (born 1948) became the first person in musical history to have six shows running simultaneously in London's West End.

First million-selling single
Vesti la giubba, Enrico Caruso

Caruso (1873–1921) was an outstanding Italian tenor and his recording of 'On with the motley' from Leoncavallo's opera *I Pagliacci* became the first ever record to sell more than one million copies.

Fastest-selling single
Candle in the Wind (1997) Elton John

The 1997 version of 'Candle in the Wind', written by Elton John and Bernie Taupin, is a reworking of their earlier tribute to film star Marilyn Monroe, now dedicated to Diana, Princess of Wales. The record sold over 600,000 copies on its day of release, 13 September 1997.

Biggest-selling single
Candle in the Wind (1997)

Over 31 million copies were sold worldwide in one month. See also Fastest-selling single, p.234. The previous holder of this record was the 1942 Bing Crosby version of Irving Berlin's 'White Christmas', which has sold a total of 30 million copies worldwide.

Biggest-selling single in the UK

See Biggest-selling single above.

First single to sell over 2 million in the UK
Mull of Kintyre (1977) Paul McCartney and Wings

Biggest-selling album
Thriller (1982) Michael Jackson
45 million copies

Biggest-selling solo singer
Elvis Presley

Presley (1935–77) had 14 consecutive million-selling

hits and sold some 500 million records during his lifetime. Over 20 million records were sold in the 24 hours after his death. He was the most successful recording artist ever known.

Biggest-selling UK solo singer
Elton John

Elton John, born Reginald Dwight in 1947, with his songwriting partner, Bernie Taupin, has enjoyed over 25 years of success, with hit songs every year in both the UK and USA.

Most successful group
The Beatles

The Beatles (John Lennon, Paul McCartney, Ringo Starr and George Harrison) were part of the 1960s 'Merseybeat' sound from Liverpool and were formed in 1960. They soon developed their own style and the Lennon–McCartney songwriting partnership became the most successful in history. 'Love Me Do' was their first hit in 1962. The group dominated pop music during the sixties and soon achieved international fame. The Beatles were awarded 47 gold discs, and their total record sales worldwide are estimated to be more than a billion. The 'Fab Four' split in 1970 and Lennon was shot and killed in New York in 1980. Of the remaining members, Paul McCartney has been the most consistently musically successful, and has forged his own career with his group Wings. He has also composed a classical work, *Standing Stone*, which was performed at the Royal Albert Hall in 1997.

Most number 1 singles
17 Elvis Presley, The Beatles

Largest sculpture
Stone Mountain heads, Georgia, USA

The faces of the American Civil War Confederate generals Robert E. Lee and Stonewall Jackson, together with that of the Confederate president, Jefferson Davis, are carved over 800 ft (245 m) high on the side of Stone Mountain, near Decatur, Georgia. The huge faces are over 90 ft (27 m) in length and the carving took over eight years to complete, from 1963–72.

Largest sculpture in the UK
Angel of the North, near Gateshead, England

The *Angel of the North* stands on a windswept hillside beside the A1 road and the main east-coast railway line. It measures 65 ft (19.8 m) in height and has a 175 ft (53.3 m) wingspan. The artist is Anthony Gormley and the sculpture cost £800,000. Built to withstand 100 mph (160 km/h) winds, the Angel contains some 200 tons (203 tonnes) of steel, each wing weighs 50 tons (50.8 tonnes) and is held in place by 88 bolts.

Most famous statue
Statue of Liberty, New York, USA

The statue's full name is *Liberty Enlightening the World* and it was gifted to the USA by France as a symbol of friendship between the two countries. The statue is 302 ft (92 m) high and represents a female figure with a torch in her right hand and tablet, inscribed 4 July 1776 (the date of the Declaration of American Independence) in her left hand. On the base is a sonnet by Emma Lazarus which includes the famous lines:

Keep, ancient lands, your storied pomp,
Give me your tired, your poor
Your huddled masses yearning to breathe free,
The wretched refuse of your teeming shore.

The statue was the work of French sculptor Frédéric Auguste Bartholdi. It was erected in New York Harbour and dedicated by President Cleveland on 18 October 1886.

Most famous painting
Mona Lisa

Leonardo da Vinci (1452–1519) painted the *Mona Lisa* in around 1504. It is now on show in the Louvre Museum, Paris, where it is heavily guarded. Its value is impossible to assess.

Highest price paid for a painting
$82 million (£49 million)

Paid in 1990 for *Dr Gachet*, a portrait by Vincent van Gogh (1853–90).

Longest opera
Die Meistersinger von Nürnberg
5 hours

The Mastersingers of Nuremberg was composed by Richard Wagner (1813–83), who also wrote the longest opera cycle, the 15-hour *Ring of the Nibelung*.

Largest orchestral score
Gothic Symphony

Havergal Brian (1876-1972) wrote this work for an orchestra of some 200 performers and choirs of 400–600 singers.

Quietest musical performance
4 Minutes 33 Seconds
John Cage

John Cage (1912–92) was a pupil of Schoenberg. His music reveals a passion for experimentation and innovation, and his belief that all sounds are, in fact, musical sounds is manifested in *4 Minutes 33 Seconds*, in which the performers and audience sit in complete silence, aware only of the sounds around them.

Longest-running television drama production
Coronation Street
9 December 1960 to present

Longest-serving television presenter on one programme
Patrick Moore
The Sky at Night 1957 to present

First printed book (movable type)
Gutenberg Bible (1455)

Johannes Gutenberg (c. 1398–1468), in partnership with his wealthy patron, Johann Fust of Mainz,

Germany, produced what is generally accepted as being the first printed book, a Bible, in Latin. It is also known as the *42-Line Bible* and the *Mazarin Bible*. There are no page numbers and the book looks in style very much like a hand-copied book. Gutenberg is also thought to have printed a grammar book and a dictionary and while he is known for his careful and meticulous work, he made very little money from his printing. By the end of the 15th century more than 1000 printers were using presses with movable type, including William Caxton in England. See below, First printed book in English.

First printed book in English (movable type)
The History of Troy (1475)

William Caxton (c. 1422–91) translated the text from French and printed several copies of the book in response to requests from his friends. It was, however, not printed in England, but in Bruges, Belgium.

Highest-selling writer (fiction)
Agatha Christie

Agatha Christie (1890–1976) began writing while working as a nurse in World War I (1914–18). Her first novel, *The Mysterious Affair at Styles* (1920), introduced the Belgian detective, Hercule Poirot, to the world; he subsequently featured in over 25 novels and short stories. Jane Marple, the spinsterish amateur sleuth, first appeared in 1930 in *Murder at the Vicarage*. Agatha Christie's play, *The Mousetrap*, is the longest-running play ever known (see above, Longest theatrical run). Her books have been translated into 44 languages and are estimated to have sold over 2 billion copies worldwide.

Highest-selling living writer (fiction)
Barbara Cartland

Barbara Cartland (born 1901) has written over 600 books and still produces some 23 new titles each year. She writes only romantic fiction and has an estimated 600 million readers worldwide.

Highest-selling book
The Bible

Precise figures are impossible to give, but the Bible is thought to have sold over five billion copies worldwide; it has been translated into 350 languages.

Oldest national daily newspaper in the UK

The Times
Founded 1788

Daily newspaper with highest number of UK readers

The Sun
Founded 1969, over 4 million readers

Sunday newspaper with highest number of UK readers

News of the World
Founded 1843, over 4 million readers

Oldest periodical

Philosophical Transactions of the Royal Society
Founded 1665

The Royal Society of London for the Promotion of Natural Knowledge is the oldest, and most prestigious, scientific society in Britain, founded in 1660. It received a Charter from Charles II and its achievements became immediately renowned in the scientific community. Members have included such illustrious names as Robert Hooke, Christopher Wren, Isaac Newton and Edward Halley. In 1768, the Society sponsored James Cook's expedition to the Pacific. Membership of the Royal Society remains exclusive; every candidate must have his or her application supported by several full members (Fellows). There are about 1000 Fellows and 100 foreign members.

Oldest annual publication in the UK
Old Moore's Almanac
Founded 1700

Dr Moore called his almanac *Vox Stellarum* (*Voice of the Stars*), and it is dedicated to astrological predictions and forecasts for the coming year.

Sport

Most Olympic participants
10,700 accredited athletes
Atlanta, Georgia, USA 1996

The XXVI Olympiad which ran from 19 July to 4 August 1996 in Atlanta had the largest number of participants ever recorded, one third of them women. Every invited National Olympic Committee sent a team, a total of 197 teams, the first time in history that this has happened.

Greatest number of gold medals in individual events (men)
10 Raymond Ewry, USA (track and field)

Greatest number of gold medals in individual events (women)
7 Vera Cáslavská, Czechoslovakia (gymnastics)

Most gold medals in one Olympics
7 Mark Spitz, USA, 1972 (swimming)

Most gold medals (men)
9 Paavo Nurmi, Finland (track and field)
9 Mark Spitz, USA (swimming)

Most gold medals (women)
9 Larissa Latynina, USSR (gymnastics)

Greatest number of Olympic medals (men)
15 Nikolai Andrianov, USSR (gymnastics)

Greatest number of Olympic medals (women)
18 Larissa Semyonovna, USSR (gymnastics)

Track and field (men)

100 m Donovan Bailey, Canada 9.84 sec (1996)

> NB Ben Johnson (Canada) ran slightly faster times in 1987 and 1988, but these records were disallowed following his disqualification after a positive drugs test.

200 m Michael Duane Johnson, USA 19.32 sec (1996)

400 m Butch Reynolds, USA 43.29 sec (1988)

800 m Sebastian Coe, GB 1.41.73 (1981)

1500 m Noureddine Morceli, Algeria 3.27.37 (1995)

Marathon Belayneh Dinsamo, Ethiopia 2.06.50 (1988)

High jump Javier Sotomayor, Cuba 8 ft $1/_2$ in (2.46 m) (1993)

Long jump Mike Powell, USA 29 ft $41/_2$ in (8.95 m) (1991)

Javelin Jan Zelezny, Czech Republic 323 ft 1 in (98.48 m) (1996)

Track and field (women)

100 m Florence Griffith Joyner, USA 10.49 sec (1988)

200 m Florence Griffith Joyner, USA 21.34 sec (1988)

400 m Marita Koch, GDR 47.60 sec (1985)

800 m Jarmila Kratochvilová, Czechoslovakia 1.53.28 (1983)

1500 m Qu Yunxia, China 3.50.46 (1993)

Marathon Ingrid Kristiansen, Norway 2.21.06 (1985)

High jump Stefka Kostadinova, Bulgaria 6 ft 10$^1/_4$ in (2.09 m) (1987)

Long jump Galina Chistakova, USSR 24 ft 8$^1/_4$ in (7.52 m) (1988)

Javelin Petra Felke, GDR 262 ft 5 in (79.98 m) (1988)

Football

First World Cup winner
Uruguay, 1930

Most World Cup wins
4 Brazil

Most English Football League Championships
18 Liverpool

Most Scottish Football League Championships
47 Rangers

Most Football Association Cup wins
9 Manchester United

Rugby

Most Rugby League Championships
17 Wigan

Most Challenge Cup wins
16 Wigan

Most Rugby Union Five Nations Championship wins (post-war)
11 England

Most Grand Slam wins (winning all four matches)
11 England

Most Triple Crown wins
20 England

Cricket

Most county cricket outright wins
29 Yorkshire

Highest individual batting score
501 runs
Brian Lara, Warwickshire v Durham, 1994

Highest individual English Test batting score
375 runs
Brian Lara, West Indies v England, 1993/4

Oldest Test player
52 yrs 165 days
Wilfred Rhodes, England

Youngest Test player
15 yrs 124 days
Mushtaq Mohammad, Pakistan

Tennis

Most men's Wimbledon titles
13 Hugh 'Laurie' Doherty, GB

Most women's Wimbledon titles
20 Billie-Jean King, USA

Most men's Wimbledon singles titles
5 Björn Borg, Sweden

Most women's Wimbledon singles titles
9 Martina Navratilova, USA

COLLINS GEM

Bestselling Collins Gem titles include:

Gem English Dictionary (£3.99)

Gem Thesaurus (£3.99)

Gem French Dictionary (£3.99)

Gem German Dictionary (£3.99)

Gem Calorie Counter (£3.50)

Gem Basic Facts Mathematics (£3.99)

Gem SAS Survival Guide (£3.99)

Gem Babies' Names (£3.50)

Gem Card Games (£3.99)

Gem Ready Reference (£3.99)

All Collins Gems are available from your local bookseller or can be ordered directly from the publishers.

In the UK, contact Mail Order, Dept 2A, HarperCollins Publishers, Westerhill Rd, Bishopbriggs, Glasgow, G64 2QT, listing the titles required and enclosing a cheque or p.o. for the value of the books plus £1.00 for the first title and 25p for each additional title to cover p&p. Access and Visa cardholders can order on 0141-772 2281 (24 hr).

In Australia, contact Customer Services, HarperCollins Distribution, Yarrawa Rd, Moss Vale 2577 (tel. [048] 68 0300). **In New Zealand**, contact Customer Services, HarperCollins Publishers, 31 View Rd, Glenfield, Auckland 10 (tel. [09] 444 3740). **In Canada**, contact your local bookshop.

All prices quoted are correct at time of going to press.

COLLINS GEM